Corporate Culture and the Quality Organization

Corporate Culture and the Quality Organization

James W. Fairfield-Sonn

Foreword by Lawrence K. Williams

Q

QUORUM BOOKS
Westport, Connecticut • London

Library of Congress Cataloging-in-Publication Data

Fairfield-Sonn, James W., 1948–
   Corporate culture and the quality organization /
James W. Fairfield-Sonn ; foreword by Lawrence K. Williams.
     p.   cm.
   Includes bibliographical references and index.
   ISBN 0–89930–903–8 (alk. paper)
    1. Total quality management. 2. Corporate culture. I. Title.
HD62.15.F35 2001
658.4′013—dc21   00–032809

British Library Cataloguing in Publication Data is available.

Library of Congress Catalog Card Number: 00–032809
ISBN: 0–89930–903–8

First published in 2001

Quorum Books, 88 Post Road West, Westport, CT 06881
An imprint of Greenwood Publishing Group, Inc.
www.quorumbooks.com

Printed in the United States of America

The paper used in this book complies with the
Permanent Paper Standard issued by the National
Information Standards Organization (Z39.48–1984).

10 9 8 7 6 5 4 3 2 1

Dedicated to my wife, Lynn, and
children, Anne, James, and John

Contents

Figures

Foreword

A German philosopher concluded an extremely long letter by apologizing for its length and explaining that he did not know enough about the subject to write a short letter. Jim Fairfield-Sonn has written a short and concise book, and clearly he understands the subject matter: corporate culture and quality improvement.

The early chapters of the book explain organizational culture in a manner that is understandable to all of its intended audiences. I wish very much that it had been available many years ago when, as a consultant, I was shown a memo by a potential client who had received a directive from his chief executive officer (CEO). The CEO had returned from a two-day retreat at a fancy resort and had requested that the personnel department have a strong culture in place by the end of the fiscal year!

The author does an effective job of tracing the use of culture as an organizational concept from the writings of Peters and Waterman (1982) to more contemporary uses, particularly in the case of mergers and acquisitions. Chapter 2 is an equally good read for students of organizational behavior, CEOs, or members of their boards. While many authors use culture as an explanatory variable, few provide help in measuring or evaluating culture. Fairfield-Sonn's discussion on measuring culture and cultural differences is one of the very solid contributions of this book.

The various approaches to continuous quality improvement are quite thoroughly examined. Most interesting is the thoughtful overview of the gurus of quality improvement: Deming, Juran, and Crosby. Most contemporary authors give these pioneers short shrift but, as Fairfield-Sonn points out, they anticipated most of the problems that have arisen and the solutions that are in place today. Perhaps their biggest failing was their somewhat heavy-handed proscriptions and prescriptions. The book also contains an up-to-date discussion of the Malcolm Baldrige Quality Awards. The most recent changes in criteria for allocating the awards are noted. The new emphasis on bottom-line results should mute some of the criticisms of this program.

Several of the chapters in Part II, "Making Quality Happen," benefit from case descriptions that are taken from Fairfield-Sonn's 20 years of consulting practice. The cases come from different industries and from both the private and nonprofit sectors. There are vignettes from such giants as General Electric and Fidelity Investments, as well as from some very much smaller firms. The description of continuous quality improvement at Connecticut Renaissance, which provides drug rehabilitation services, adds a very distinctive touch to this book.

The chapter on rewarding performance undoubtedly contains one of the most vital messages in the book for any organization that is planning a quality improvement program. Citing Steve Kerr's 1975 article, "On the Folly of Rewarding A, While Hoping for B," Fairfield-Sonn provides examples from his own and others experiences that demonstrate the importance of continuous, top-level involvement and a comprehensive reward system that reinforces the vision of long-range, continuous improvement.

As the author points out, with so many American firms focused almost solely on the next quarter, it is not an accident that Japanese firms, with their extended view of the future, were pioneers in the area of continuous quality improvement.

Jim Fairfield-Sonn has been a very successful consultant in addition to being an effective and popular professor. Jim's success in both endeavors is due, in part, to his self-effacing manner that allows the student and the client to take full credit for their accomplishments. This same unassuming manner comes through in the text in a very pleasant way. This book involves the author as observer and stays away from the ego-inflating stories that get in the way of so many of the volumes in this general topic area. I am delighted that Jim, a former student, asked me to write this foreword. This is truly a book I wish I had written.

Lawrence K. Williams,
Professor Emeritus,
Cornell University,
Ithaca, New York

Preface

It has been known for some time that the quality of products and services offered by a firm is one of the best predictors of long-term organizational performance. Given this fact, it would make sense for continuous quality improvement to be one of the top priorities of all organizations. Yet, in reality, we know that firms vary widely in the level of quality that they aspire to offer to their customers as well as how well they deliver on whatever promises they make.

Why do some firms provide higher-quality goods and services than others? Many thoughts have been offered over the years. In studying firms that have consistently improved their quality over time, however, common patterns emerge. In other words, improving quality is not a mysterious process. Rather, the success of these companies can be traced back to a set of disciplined activities that they routinely engage in and work hard at doing well, albeit in somewhat different ways. These disciplined activities allow them to gain a competitive edge.

The aim of this book is to identify and illustrate those core activities that are repeatedly associated with successful quality improvement efforts. Given its intent, this book is different from most others in the field in three important respects. First, the goal here is neither to explore one quality improvement method in great depth nor to provide a comprehensive list of the many ways that firms have attempted to improve quality. These approaches are already well represented in the literature. Instead, here attention is directed only at a carefully selected set of quality drivers consistently seen across a wide spectrum of firms. In this way, regardless of the industry that readers work in, they will benefit from understanding where and how the greatest gain from investments in quality are likely to be realized.

Second, most books in the quality field emphasize the tools and techniques for bringing about a technical change. While these tools and techniques are critical to the success of the effort, the emphasis in this book is on understanding why bringing about a cultural change is even more important. The reason for this emphasis is simple. Experience in the field has convinced the author that once a continuous improvement culture has been established, it is relatively easy to teach the tools and techniques to make quality improvements. On the other hand, if the culture is not supportive of the effort, then training in the tools and techniques is a waste of time and money.

Third, while there are many important ingredients in the recipe for success, there are also more and less effective ways to approach the change effort. In other words, not just the ingredients but also how they are added to the batter determine how well the cake will look and taste. For example, beginning the quality journey by training employees on how to improve their work processes and then expecting it to just happen will lead to a disappointing end product. Rather, significant quality improvement will come only after the senior management team has established a sound platform for the whole organization to move forward on a strategic quality improvement agenda. Then, the senior management team must consciously allocate resources to make it happen as well as visibly support the development of a disciplined approach to making quality improvement a way of life for everyone in the organization.

AUDIENCES

This book is aimed at three primary audiences: executives who are responsible for improving the quality of the products and services offered by their firm; external and internal consultants who are actively involved in helping others to improve their work systems, processes, and procedures; and academics and students who are interested in learning more about how others have been able to improve the quality of the goods and services that they deliver. While each of these audiences brings a different perspective and set of questions to the book, they will all benefit from seeing in the end that continuous quality improvement is as much about creating a supportive quality culture within an organization as learning how to appropriately use a growing set of quality improvement tools and techniques.

OVERVIEW OF THE CONTENT

This book is organized in three parts. Part I provides a broad overview on how to start thinking about creating a quality organization. The discussion begins by asking the critical question, How much quality is enough? The answer to that question leads into a discussion of why and how quality standards have evolved and where they are headed in the future. Then, attention is directed at explaining why creating a supportive culture is so important to the success of a continuous quality improvement effort. This Part concludes with a review of how to create a foundation for an integrated quality improvement effort and how the Malcolm Baldrige National Quality Award program can help firms to get started on, or enhance their efforts along, the quality journey.

Part II explores how to drive a quality improvement effort into an organization, the first key task being to make quality improvement a key strategic priority. Next, some ideas are presented on how to make a firm more customer-focused. Then, a general outline is provided for how to structure the rollout of a formal quality improvement program. The last two chapters in this Part suggest ways to enhance employee involvement in the quality effort by aligning their long-term professional and personal development needs with participation in the program as well as ensuring that short-term recognition and rewards are provided.

Part III examines a number of emerging quality issues. Specifically, Chapter 9 takes a closer look at how some firms are now proactively taking steps to foster a richer learning environment within the firm as well as pursuing partnerships with other organizations as a way to improve the quality of their own products and services. Chapter 10 looks at the implications stemming from the drive toward six sigma levels of quality and what new opportunities are being made available from advances in information technology. The book concludes with a summary of the lessons learned and an invitation to others to join or rejoin the quality journey.

Acknowledgments

Writing this book has been a collaborative effort. Without the insights gained and helpful feedback received from many clients, colleagues, and students in my seminar on process and project management this book would not have become a reality. Thus, I want to begin by expressing my appreciation to everyone who has been involved in shaping the ideas contained here.

As often happens, however, some individuals make greater contributions than others. Accordingly, I would like to identify a number of individuals who were particularly helpful in bringing this work to completion. Some of these individuals have been invaluable in clarifying the general ideas presented in this book, and others made a major contribution by providing specific examples to demonstrate the potential of quality improvement efforts to enhance the competitiveness of organizations and the work lives of individuals. A third group of colleagues was instrumental in helping to improve the presentation of the ideas themselves.

In terms of clarifying the ideas presented here, I want to express particular appreciation to Paul Bacdayan, Paul Carpenter, Sheila Carmine, Mary Carsky, Steve Congden, Steve Darter, David Miller, Sandra Morgan, and Dick Raspa, who read and commented on drafts of this work. In addition, I want to recognize the excellent research support provided by Josh Lowy, Bryant McConkie, and Pinkesh Patel whose tireless and enthusiastic efforts uncovered many illustrations of how quality concepts are being converted into useful applications across a wide range of industries.

A personal note of thanks also goes to several colleagues and friends who generously provided information for several of the in-depth case studies presented in the book. These contributors include Joel Becker, Chairman and CEO of Torrington Supply Company; Patrick McAuliffe, Executive Director, Connecticut Renaissance; and Laura Groark, Vice President, Fidelity Investments. All of their organizations embody many of the quality principles and practices described in this book. Working closely with, or observing, their organizations over the last several years as they move forward on the quality journey has been a source of great personal and professional pleasure and inspiration.

Third, I want to thank several individuals who graciously offered their time and talents to help enhance the presentation of the ideas in this book. In particular, special thanks go to Denise Eltouny of Yale University and Helmi Cotter at the University of Hartford as well as Lynn Taylor and Hilary Claggett at Greenwood Publishing.

Finally, I would like to acknowledge my appreciation to several individuals who helped me to get to this point in my career. Without their invaluable support at critical points in my professional development, I would not be writing this book at this time. Foremost among these individuals are Larry Williams, Cornell's School of Industrial and Labor Relations, who introduced me to the joys of doing field research; Allen Kraut, who while at IBM showed me how to rigorously apply theory to the solution of practical problems; and Clayton Alderfer, my dissertation chair at Yale's School of Organization and Management, who guided me through my first in-depth study of the influence of culture on organizational performance. Their help and inspiration have truly made a significant difference in my life and thinking, for which I will be forever grateful.

Part I

The Quest for Quality

Chapter 1

How Much Quality Is Enough?

Our thinking creates problems that the same type of thinking will not solve.

—Albert Einstein

As Albert Einstein so wisely pointed out, many of our problems can be traced back directly to how we think about things. While this sage insight is useful in many areas of life, it is invaluable for anyone responsible for building a quality organization, helping someone else to build a quality organization, or studying how quality organizations are built. The reason that this idea can be so useful in building a quality organization is that this effort demands a willingness to challenge a great deal of conventional knowledge and the flexibility to adopt new strategies and new structures and, most importantly, to nurture a new culture to support a fundamentally different way of running an organization. As you will see throughout this book, the effort required to become a quality-driven company is substantial. On the other hand, if a firm is intent on thriving for the long term, the rewards are well worth it.

EVOLVING QUALITY STANDARDS

One of the first questions that surface in thinking about building a quality organization is, How much quality will be enough? This is a critical question to ask because extensive market research (Buzzell and Gale, 1987; Hamel and Prahalad, 1994; Kotler, Jatusripitak, and Maesincee, 1997) has shown that when it comes to profitability, quality is king. That is, across a wide range of industries it has been consistently found that firms perceived as being quality leaders based on the nature of their products and services have historically been the most profitable. Thus, quality leadership is simply the best path to long-term, sustainable success.

Yet knowing that quality is important to the success of an organization, in general, still does not answer the question, What level of quality should any specific firm pursue? The answer to that question can be determined only after analyzing the dynamic interplay of three factors that are critical in determining quality standards within an industry and then deciding how to respond to them. First, what level of quality are competing organizations in my industry capable of delivering? Second, how much supply and demand exist for my products and services in the market at any given time? Third, what are interested third parties saying about the overall quality of the products and services being provided by my industry?

More precisely, the first question that needs to be addressed is, How much capacity do rival firms currently have to deliver high-quality goods and services? In making this assessment, it is important to distinguish hopes from reality. That is, while many organizations say that they are striving for perfection, in fact, internal systems capabilities set limits for how well any firm can perform. Knowing how well competing firms will actually deliver on their promises is critical to setting your own quality standards.

The second major influence on the quality standards that needs to be considered is how much supply and demand currently exist for a given product or service. Experience has shown that consumers are willing to accept lower than desired quality during times of emergency such as during a war or in the wake of natural disasters. On the other hand, when supply outstrips demand, which is increasingly characteristic of markets around the world, then competitive pressures mount to increase quality standards, and the customer becomes king.

For example, during a recent trip to Poland, a faculty member at a major university explained to the author (Fairfield-Sonn and Lacey, 1996) that during the Russian occupation the state-controlled economy could not produce enough goods to meet consumers' demands. So, among other things, there were chronic food shortages. As a result, when you went to the grocery store to buy something like a bottle of vinegar, none might be available. What could a customer do? After waiting a long time in a line, if you wanted to buy anything, it might be necessary to settle for a bottle of oil. Now if this shopping experience irritated you, she explained that it was wise not to share your feelings with the store clerk because he thought you were lucky to get anything. To make matters worse, the only place to register a formal complaint was with the government, but since the government also controlled the means of production and the press, that was likewise not a prudent thing to do. Now that goods are more available in Poland and a more open and responsive government is running the country, however, this type of experience would be considered to be totally unacceptable.

The third factor to consider in setting quality standards for a firm is, What are interested third parties saying about quality standards in the industry? Foremost among these groups are government consumer protection agencies, which have legislative mandates to monitor and enforce quality standards. Another major group to be aware of is consumer advocates coming from the ranks of socially conscious observers and critics of business practices. These writers, such as Upton Sinclair, whose book *The Jungle* (1906) provided a devastating exposé of the ghastly practices in the Chicago slaughterhouses at the time, and Ralph Nader, whose book *Unsafe at Any Speed* (1966) offered a disturbing look at how safety decisions were being made by major automobile manufacturers, have had a powerful influence on raising quality standards by revealing the shady side of some business practices. Yet another influential group of interested third parties comes to the issue of quality standards from an evaluation and information-sharing perspective. Notable examples here include the Consumers Union, publisher of *Consumer Reports*, and J.D. Powers and Associates, whose quality ratings have had a significant impact on both buying patterns and production standards.

In summary, a useful starting point for thinking about how to build a quality organization is to recognize that quality standards have and will fluctuate over time based on changes in the capacity of rival organizations to produce varying levels of quality in their goods and services; market conditions; and the indirect influence of interested third parties. Thus, determining what constitutes an acceptable level of quality will always be a moving target. It is equally important to note that the trend has been for quality standards, in general, to increase and for variation across products and services to decrease (Carsky, Dickinson, and Canedy, 1998). So, to be competitive, a firm must know what quality standards currently exist and then set out to beat them.

QUALITY STANDARD 1: MEETING CUSTOMER EXPECTATIONS

In the remainder of this introductory chapter, we explore some of the most thought-provoking ideas and recommendations that have been offered on the subject of how to meet ever-higher quality standards. This discussion begins with detailed advice given by the three most prominent early writers on quality improvement, namely, W. Edwards Deming, Joseph Juran, and Philip Crosby, whose primary focus was on helping firms to meet customer expectations.

Their pioneering work is important because collectively they created the foundation for the quality revolution that blossomed in the 1980s (Gale, 1994). After reviewing the seminal thoughts of these three giants in the field, attention turns to ways to think about pursuing even higher levels of quality aimed at exceeding customer expectations and delighting customers. The chapter concludes with a review of the thoughts of executives from four major firms on why they decided to make a commitment to becoming a totally quality- and process- driven organization.

W. Edwards Deming

The growing drive toward continuous quality improvement as we know it today can be traced directly back to the ground-breaking work of W. Edwards Deming in the 1950s. Deming, who is widely referred to as the "Father of the American Quality Movement," was trained as a statistician. During World War II he refined much of his thinking on how to improve quality in defense production operations. After the war, however, he was disappointed to find very little receptivity to his ideas in the United States. This rejection was not hard to understand. America had won the war and was the only major nation not to suffer serious physical damage from the war. As a result, while most of the major countries around the world were trying to rebuild their plants, in America the problem was how to produce enough goods and services, of whatever quality, to satisfy a vast domestic and worldwide demand.

Given worldwide economic conditions at the time, it is not surprising to find that Deming's influence was not felt first in the United States. Rather, his first opportunity to test out the full power of his ideas was in Japan. Struggling to overcome the devastating effects of losing the war, in the 1950s Japan was in a shambles. What few products it could produce were of shoddy quality, and "made in Japan" was a bad joke. Nonetheless, when Japanese business leaders within the Union of Japanese Science and Engineering (JUSE) heard of Deming's ideas, they invited him to come and share his ideas with them. He went, stayed several years, and shared his wisdom, and for his efforts the JUSE created the Deming Prize for Quality in his honor. The rest is history.

What Deming had been working on was a whole new theory of management based on optimizing the operation of the whole system through statistical control (Deming, 1986, 1982). His belief was that in order to achieve quality improvement, it would be necessary for most firms to adopt a new management philosophy and implement an associated set of new business practices. Working with this new philosophy and set of practices, he felt strongly that it would be possible to instill the desire and create the capacity to develop what he called a continuous quality improvement work environment within any firm, that is, a firm where every process from manufacturing to recruiting was being continually examined to discover ways to make it more effective and efficient. To be successful in the endeavor, however, organizations would need to begin changing both their management culture and the techniques that they used to get work done.

To convey the magnitude of the cultural changes needed to bring about a transformation to continuous quality improvement to a wide range of audiences, Deming summarized the essence of his ideas in two simple, yet powerful, ways. One approach was a schematic diagram that came to be known as "Deming's chain reaction." The other was his "14 points." The most critical points contained in each of these two guides to the quality journey are detailed next.

Deming's chain reaction model (Figure 1.1) appears simple on the surface, but at its heart are two challenging core assumptions that continue to be the subject of considerable debate even today. One assumption, accepted more easily in theory than in practice, is that the job of leaders and managers, in particular, is to optimize the whole system. This belief stands in sharp contrast to the openly stated or unconscious position of many in management who feel that their job should be focused on maximizing departmental or personal outcomes from a job. Deming's second assumption was that the primary goal of senior management should be to improve the performance of the whole organization over the long term rather than to maximize short-term, quarterly results.

Deming's position stood in bold contrast to the prevailing wisdom of the 1950s, as it still does in many firms today. Yet, he was also aware that he was not talking merely about a matter of independent, individual choice. Leaders and managers, regardless of their personal power and influence, work within the context of a larger system. When that system rewards individuals for self-serving, short-term behavior, that is the type of behavior individuals will engage in. This is why he felt that the culture and the reward structure of the whole firm had to change, or no significant impact would be seen.

Figure 1.1
Deming's Chain Reaction

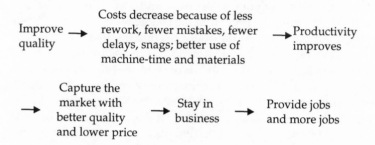

Source: W.E. Deming, *Out of the Crisis* (Cambridge: MIT Center for Advanced Engineering Study), 1986, p. 3. Used with permission.

The logic behind Deming's chain reaction is relatively straightforward. Yet, as noted, it was revolutionary when he first presented it in the 1950s and remains controversial today. The heart of the debate centers around the first two steps in the chain reaction.

When Deming first introduced this model in the 1950s, many firms believed that the best way to improve a firm's overall profitability was to focus on decreasing costs. Deming vehemently disagreed with this premise. He argued that any efforts aimed primarily at cost reduction would inevitably have a negative impact on the quality of an organization's goods and services and thereby precipitate or further accelerate the firm's decline.

In addition, he objected to these cuts because they would often pit manager against manager in budget wars and thus reinforce the tendency to put departmental or individual wellbeing above the needs of the larger organization. Across-the-board cuts were no better because while they might generate short-term savings, everyone was hurt to the same degree. In other words, through the use of nondiscriminating cuts managers were being taught that it doesn't matter how much good you do for the organization; in the end everyone will be punished equally. When this type of thinking settles in, it can be demoralizing, and the organization as a whole will become the loser in the long run (Aguayo, 1990).

Deming's recommendation to senior management, therefore, was always to start by first improving the quality of the organization's current systems, processes, and procedures. If these could be improved, he argued in his classic work *Out of the Crisis* (1986), then costs would naturally decline because there would be less rework, less scrap, less need to offer warranties, and so on. He was likewise ardent in advocating that it was not necessary to invest in expensive new machinery or materials to begin realizing savings. Indeed, based on substantial experience in the field, he believed that in many cases a major root cause of poor current performance was the underutilization of existing resources. So, before investing in new resources, which would be expensive and disrupt ongoing production efforts, first spend time removing as much variation as possible from the present system. When this phase of the improvement effort was completed, it might or might not be necessary to move on to other capital investments.

Once the existing system is stabilized, then management should embark on a concerted effort to make additional process improvements that result in further quality enhancement. These enhancements, in turn, will yield more cost savings.

As quality improves and costs decline, productivity will also improve because it is no longer necessary to take the time and resources to fix defective goods or recover from a bad service experience.

Increasing productivity, in turn, means that it is less expensive for a firm to make goods or offer services. Thus, they can be offered at a lower cost, and the organization can still make reasonable profits. This will lead to increased market share as customers come to realize over time that they can buy higher-quality goods and services at lower cost from your firm as opposed to the competition.

This leads to the best news for employees and investors, namely, that the firm gets to stay in business and create more and more jobs.

In addition to the chain reaction model, Deming's other major means of communicating his new philosophy was through the articulation of what he called "14 Points." These points provide a broad outline of a quality improvement change program that he believed would provide the basis for the transformation of American industry as he saw it at that time. They include the following key points, which have been the subject of considerable scrutiny and debate for decades.

1. *Create constancy of purpose for improvement of product and service.* Every organization must deal with two classes of problems: today's problems and those to be faced sometime in the future. To create a quality organization, senior management's primary focus must be on long- term issues that the firm will need to address 10, 20, or 30 years from now. That is, customers, suppliers, and employees of a firm must know that prudent investments in new product development, employee education, and research are being made today that will ensure that the firm will be there for them well into the future.

2. *Adopt the new philosophy.* In our emerging global economy, firms will no longer be competitive if current levels of mistakes are accepted, if material not suited for the job is shipped, if people are untrained for their jobs, if there is inadequate or ineffective supervision, if people jobhop, and if the government continues to create obstacles to competition. A new philosophy based on all 14 points is necessary to turn the tide.

3. *Cease dependence on mass inspection.* One hundred percent inspection is the equivalent of planning for defects. You cannot inspect quality into a product. After a product is made, you cannot put quality into it. The only way to improve quality is to build it into the production process.

4. *End the practice of awarding business on the basis of price tag alone.* Price has no meaning absent an associated measure of quality. Selecting a supplier based solely on who offers the lowest price is a bad business practice. Rather, purchasing decisions should be made

on the basis of the *lowest total cost*, which includes an evaluation of the quality of the product or service that will be received along with the price. Changing suppliers just to get a lower price is likewise a bad business practice. It costs time and money to learn how to use the goods and services provided by a new supplier. A better approach is to develop long-term relationships with only a few suppliers who are also committed to continuously improving their products and services.

5. *Improve constantly and forever the system of production and service.* Focusing on improving the quality of a product or service misses the real point of continuous quality improvement. Significant quality enhancement comes only from improving the processes of production, the materials used in the process, the machinery involved in the process, and the knowledge of the individuals who complete the process.

6. *Institute training.* In order to improve the system, managers need to learn how to run a whole company, not just their area of responsibility. This means that every manager must know how the final product moves through the company from the receipt of raw materials, through production, to how it will be used by customers. At the same time, workers need to be trained in how to most effectively complete their assignments.

7. *Adopt and institute leadership.* Managers need to become leaders. Leaders are concerned with improving the entire work system. This is best done by reducing the common causes of poor performance. When management improves the system, workers can become more effective at doing their jobs.

8. *Drive out fear.* Workers must be secure enough in their jobs that they can raise questions to management without worrying about the potential negative consequences. When workers are fearful, they will do what they need to do to protect themselves. This is not always the same as doing what is best for the company. Remove fear, and the company as a whole will prosper.

9. *Break down barriers between staff areas.* When individuals know only their own area of functional expertise, it limits their potential contribution to the solution of organization-wide problems. Creating customer-focused, cross-functional teams consisting of

representatives from design, manufacturing, sales, service, and credit will lead to significant improvements in quality.

10. *Eliminate slogans, exhortations, and targets for the workforce.* Slogans, exhortations, and targets do not improve quality or productivity because they are aimed at the wrong people. Workers usually do the best that they can given the tools and resources provided by management. To improve performance, management needs to address the sources of common production failures.

11. *Eliminate numerical quotas for the workforce and numerical goals for management.* Numerical quotas for the workforce are counter-productive because they are aimed at increasing the quantity of work completed, not the quality. Quota systems are bad because they do not provide incentives to improve the work process; they provide incentives only to come as close as possible to the acceptable average level of production. Piecework is worse because it actually rewards the production of defective parts and the generation of scrap. Likewise, goals for management are counter-productive because they tend to focus on the quantity of output rather than how to improve the system.

12. *Remove barriers that rob people of pride of workmanship.* What workers want most in a job is the chance to do good work. Managers need to listen to employee concerns and take action to eliminate anything standing in the way of doing a good job. To do this, however, managers must understand the whole production process and be willing and able to take appropriate steps to remedy problems that surface.

13. *Encourage education and self-improvement for everyone.* An organization needs people who are improving through education. There is an abundance of good people in the world, but to improve, they need to grow in their knowledge. This knowledge is not limited to how they can do their specific job better today but also includes how they can make a larger contribution to the firm and society in the future.

14. *Take action to accomplish the transformation.* Adopting this new philosophy takes courage and determination. Changing systems is not easy work, but it is the only path to greater quality, productivity, and pride in workmanship. A path can be laid out,

and progress can be monitored, evaluated, and adjusted based on observed feedback from the effort.

In summary, Deming felt that his major contribution to the improvement of quality would come from the adoption of his new philosophy of management, specifically, that a firm's quality can be directly linked back to decisions being made by management and that these decisions reflect major cultural norms about how best to run an organization. To improve quality, therefore, you need to address deep cultural issues. Change the culture, and quality can improve. In the absence of cultural change, nothing of much significance will happen. In practice, however, he was probably better known for the new set of statistical tools and techniques that he brought to bear to show others how they could go about the actual work of improving goods and services. More is said about this in Chapter 6.

Joseph M. Juran

Shortly after Deming arrived in Japan, he was followed by another American, Joseph Juran, who would make contributions second only to Deming's in transforming the Japanese economy. This quality improvement pioneer would also go on to significantly influence the thinking of many firms around the world about how they could improve their quality. Juran's contribution to the quest for quality improvement, however, came from a different perspective, namely, a financial perspective. In addition, he provided a unifying guiding principle called "fitness for use," which he believed would provide better everyday guidance for how to move forward on the quality improvement agenda (Juran, 1988).

In other words, while Deming was a philosopher and a statistician, Juran brought a more practical, day-to-day perspective to the business of improving quality. So, while audiences listening to Deming typically heard the call to change their management philosophy and to improve internal processes throughout the firm by the use of statistical process controls, from Juran they heard a slightly different message.

Juran's message was more focused on getting the biggest return on investment for resources devoted to improving processes. That is, as a practical matter, it needs to be recognized that all process improvement efforts are not equally important for a firm. Depending on what strategy a firm is pursuing, its target customer population, and the internal capabilities of the firm at any given time, a unique ordering of process improvement priorities will emerge. This priority list, in turn, should become the guide for carefully evaluating and selecting process improvement efforts.

In addition, Juran argued that processes should *not* be continually improved. Instead, a rigorous cost-benefit analysis should be used to reveal when any given process has been sufficiently improved, and then the effort should be stopped, the ending point being determined by calculating where the costs (e.g., time, personnel, materials) associated with further improvement begin to exceed the potential benefits. As the reader will soon see, this hard-nosed, numbers-driven approach was slightly different from Deming's approach and in stark contrast to the one popularized by our third pioneer, Philip Crosby, who attracted considerable attention with his call for the pursuit of zero defects and the bold assertion that quality is free.

More precisely, to gain a handle on where to focus the quality improvement effort, Juran advocated the use of a cost-of-quality, COQ, accounting system to determine where a firm was experiencing its greatest costs due to poor quality, so these areas could become the top-priority items for improvement. To make this determination, Juran felt that four costs needed to be considered.

One cost he called "internal failure costs." These costs stem from costs of defects discovered before shipment and include items such as scrap, rework, downtime, and disposition (i.e., time devoted to determining the root cause of problems and what to do about them).

He labeled another cost "external failure costs." These costs become evident only after a product is shipped. Prominent costs in this area include complaint adjustments, cost of returned materials, warranty charges, and allowances.

A third category of costs were "appraisal costs." These costs include inspection of incoming materials, tests and inspections conducted during the production process, maintaining the accuracy of test equipment, and the ongoing evaluation of stock in inventory to ensure that it is still in good condition.

The fourth category was "prevention costs." These costs are associated with activities commonly required to run a quality program such as the annual planning effort, training, process control efforts, and quality reporting.

With knowledge of these quality costs, Juran felt that the management team could then focus on its primary responsibility, which was to minimize the total costs of quality and to determine when to stop an improvement effort because the costs had begun to exceed the benefits from improving the process. Given this approach to monitoring and improving quality, it is easy to see why Juran consistently urged firms to focus initially on "breakthrough" process improvements opportunities. These opportunities would yield a significant, short-term return for the effort, and zero defects, while desirable in theory, were an impractical quality goal because the drive toward perfection would result in an exponential increase in appraisal and prevention costs that would no longer justify the effort.

The second distinguishing aspect of Juran's approach to quality improvement was his insistence that quality means "fitness for use." That is, a product or service is fit for use only if the customer can count on it to do what she or he wanted it to do. For example, a manufacturer must make components that meet customers' production specifications.

To pursue a "fitness for use" quality program that spans the entire production process from receipt of supplies to customer complaint handling, Juran felt that five major dimensions of the production process needed to be monitored and addressed as needed.

The first key dimension is the quality of design. For instance, firms need to be clear about what level of product or service they are trying to create. Building a Rolls Royce calls for a different level of design concept and specifications from that of a Toyota.

Second, firms need to be concerned about the quality of conformance, in other words, the degree to which the quality of the product or service produced matches the tolerance requirements used in the production processes of the purchaser.

Third, there is the question of availability or the reliability and maintainability of the products and services.

The fourth dimension of concern should be safety as reflected in the potential risk of injuries associated with using the product or service.

Finally, there must be a concern for field use or understanding how the product or service will actually be used by the customer. For example, operating a jeep in temperate climates is different from running it in Alaska.

As noted earlier, given his practical bent, Juran urged firms to begin their quality programs by pursuing breakthrough projects. After these efforts had been successful in harvesting much of the low-hanging fruit, however, Juran felt that a second phase should be launched. He called this phase the "control sequence." The purpose of this phase of the quality effort was to lock in the early gains by monitoring processes with sufficient intensity that deviations in processes due to simple problems such as machines moving out of tolerance could be detected early on and quick adjustments made. When this discipline had been established, a firm could move on to the third and final phase with the establishment of annual quality programs that would make quality improvement "just the way we do business."

Philip B. Crosby

Of the three major theorists who provided the initial foundation for thinking about how to improve quality, Phil Crosby, a former vice president of quality for ITT, offered the most traditional definition of quality and the most culturally oriented approach to achieving this end. In his widely read and often cited book *Quality Is Free* (1979) Crosby defined quality simply as "conformance to requirements."

Crosby argued that quality standards are ultimately a reflection of the expectations of senior management. Therefore, if senior management believed that it was possible to achieve zero defects, then employees would come to accept this goal as their performance target. On the other hand, if senior management believed that defects are a normal part of doing business, then employees would likewise come to share this belief, and defects would never go away, that is, the quality of an organization's goods and services will never be better than what senior management believes they can be. This essentially normative approach was well received, as evidenced by the fact that from 1979 to 1985 approximately 35,000 executives and managers attended Crosby's Quality College to learn more about his ideas, and General Motors, IBM, Johnson & Johnson, and Chrysler set up their own Crosby schools.

In outlining his approach to quality improvement, Crosby was both like and unlike Deming and Juran in some important respects. He was similar to the other two quality gurus in that he directed his message primarily at senior management and believed that quality would improve only if senior managers changed their attitudes toward quality. In addition, he firmly believed that if quality improved, then costs would decrease.

He parted company with Deming and Juran, however, on what the central goal of the improvement effort should be and how best to make this happen. For Crosby, the ultimate goal was not optimizing the total system or realizing the greatest return for investment, but rather zero defects. To achieve this end, Crosby, like Juran, offered a system for measuring the cost of quality, albeit one aimed more at raising the consciousness of senior management to the true total cost of quality than picking and ending projects as Juran had done. In addition, he provided a management maturity grid for senior management to assess where they were on their quality journey and a 14-point program for making progress toward zero defects.

The management maturity grid was certainly cultural in its orientation, as it highlighted five developmental stages through which firms move as they become more aware of the impact that culture has on organizational performance. Crosby called the first phase "uncertainty." In this stage senior management does not even see quality as a management tool and so does not even know if or why quality problems exist.

The second stage he called "awakening." Here, senior management supports quality management in theory but is unwilling to commit time and resources to it. As a result, the senior management team is left wondering if the firm must always have quality problems.

Stage 3 is called "enlightenment." Here, senior management not only understands something about how quality impacts performance but for the first time becomes truly supportive of the effort and starts to identify and resolve quality problems.

The next stage Crosby called "wisdom." At this stage, senior management becomes personally involved in quality improvement efforts, and as a result the firm can begin to routinely prevent defects from occurring.

The last stage is "certainty." At this phase in its development the senior management team recognizes that quality management is essential to the success of the organization and also knows why certain actions will mean that quality problems are not happening.

To progress through these five stages, Crosby offered a 14-point plan that emphasized prevention more than corrective action. The highlights of this change program are detailed next (Crosby, 1979).

1. *Management commitment.* The first step in the program is to discuss the need for quality improvement with senior management with an emphasis on the need to prevent defects. Throughout these discussions the focus should be on communication, which will yield long-term results, as opposed to motivation, which is short-lived. The bottom line is to gain an agreement that quality improvement is a practical way to make the organization more profitable.

2. *Quality improvement team.* Representatives from each department must be brought together to form a quality improvement team. These individuals must be able to speak for their departments and be able to put the plan into action.

3. *Quality measurement.* A method must be found to measure quality throughout the organization for all key activities. Once measures are established, it will be possible to evaluate current levels of activities and build action plans for moving forward.

4. *Cost of quality evaluation.* Initial estimates of the cost of quality can be shaky, but they can be useful because they can indicate where the greatest problems exist. Having the comptroller's office establish all these measures can be useful because a uniform system will result and can be readily incorporated into other financial systems.

5. *Quality awareness.* Share with employees what nonquality is costing the organization. The aim of this effort is communicating why quality should be a concern for everyone and thereby enrolling employees in the improvement effort. This may be the most important step of all.

6. *Corrective action.* By encouraging everyone to begin discussing quality problems, solutions to obvious and not so obvious problems will arise. When problems beyond the scope of a unit are detected, they should be referred to higher levels in the organization for resolution.

7. *Establish an ad hoc committee for the zero defects program.* Several members of the ad hoc committee should be selected to explore the concept of zero defects and how it can be implemented within a department. Here the emphasis is on truly understanding what the concept of zero defects mean for the unit and how everyone can begin to do the right things the first time. It is particularly important that this effort match the personality of the unit.

8. *Supervisor training.* All levels of management need to be oriented to the program before it is officially launched. Managers must understand the program in sufficient detail so they can explain it to their people. The ability to effectively communicate the program to others is a good test of a manager's comprehension and comfort with the program.

9. *Zero Defects Day.* Establishing Zero Defects Day should be a memorable date for the whole organization. The entire organization should be introduced to the program on the same day. The goal of this effort is to make clear to everyone that zero defects is the new performance standard for the firm.

10. *Goal setting.* At the meetings each supervisor should establish 30-, 60-, and 90-day improvement goals that the unit would like to

strive for. It is important that the goals be measurable and achievable.

11. *Error cause removal*. Individuals are encouraged to describe any problem that is preventing them from doing error-free work. This is not a suggestion system but rather a way to surface problems that need attention. All of these problems should be acknowledged within 24 hours. The intent of this effort is to communicate to all employees that their concerns have been heard and that something will be done about them.

12. *Recognition*. Awards should be given to everyone who meets his or her goals or performs an outstanding act. No attempt should be made to evaluate the relative contribution of the error-cause removal effort because these efforts are not suggestions. The prizes should be in the form of recognition rather than financial.

13. *Quality councils*. The quality professionals and team chairpersons involved in the program should be brought together for periodic meetings to communicate with each other about their successes and to discuss how to move the program forward to even more solid ground.

14. *Do it over again*. A typical program might run for a year to 18 months. At that time, changes in personnel might necessitate more education and the selection of new representatives. Making Zero Defects Day an annual event will make the point that quality improvement is just a normal part of the way that the firm does its business.

QUALITY STANDARD 2: EXCEEDING CUSTOMER EXPECTATIONS

Since Deming, Juran, and Crosby were writing at a time when most American firms were facing mounting international competition and loss of market share because of the relatively poor quality of their products and services, it is not surprising that their work focused primarily on the initial goal of most quality improvement efforts, namely, to begin consistently meeting customer expectations. During the 1980s, however, in large part because of their efforts, substantial improvement was realized by many firms across a broad range of industries. With this improvement in performance, the bar for acceptable levels of quality began to rise to a higher level; namely, exceeding customer expectations became the new mark of quality excellence.

Deciding to seek this goal, however, marks a significant transition in thinking about quality for a firm because it requires moving beyond just using quality improvement as a defensive tool to its use as a strategic weapon. It also means that senior management must think about quality improvement not just as an internal matter but rather as a matter of balancing internal capacity in light of shifting customer demands. In the following, the thinking of two prominent later writers on quality improvement illustrates this evolution of thinking and the concomitant required shifts in behavior.

Compete on Specific Dimensions of Quality

When you start to think seriously about building better products or services, it is possible to quickly develop a very comprehensive list of all the characteristics that a potential customer might find desirable. An equally quick calculation of the costs associated with addressing all these issues, however, will reveal that the price for such a good or service will also probably make it prohibitively expensive to produce and sell.

How can a firm resolve this dilemma? Garvin's (1987) answer was that a company's senior management must make informed strategic choices. Specifically, in his analysis of the components of quality he identified eight relatively distinctive dimensions of quality. He argued that each of these dimensions or a combination of some of them could be used to proactively build a competitive quality strategy. On the other hand, he was equally quick to point out that trying to compete on all eight at the same time would not be the basis of a sound strategy for most firms. The eight quality dimensions are briefly discussed next.

1. *Performance*. This dimension refers to a product's basic operating characteristics. For example, in buying a car, most consumers are concerned with basic issues like how fast the car can accelerate or how well it can brake.

2. *Features*. These are the bells and whistles that can attract attention. Firms like Fidelity Investments have emphasized these in their development of specific funds aimed at health care, technology, emerging growth opportunities, and so on. In this way, individual investors can build a unique portfolio composed of stocks in industries or around business perspectives that they like or understand.

3. *Reliability*. Another concern of many consumers is how long a product can be used before it is likely to malfunction. For example, farmers have been known to want very good information on how well a machine will work during harvest times before it might malfunction.

4. *Conformance*. An issue closely related to operating characteristics is how well a product meets general specifications. This issue is particularly important in situations where two or more products need to fit together. When a number of parts need to work together, the issue of concern is called "tolerance stack-up." In other words, while each part may fall within required specifications, in combination the parts may not work or work very well. So, the tighter the overall fit, the better the performance of the final product.

5. *Durability*. This dimension refers to how much use can be expected from a product before it deteriorates. This dimension is seen in everything from how long a light bulb will last to how long an appliance such as a dishwasher or refrigerator will run.

6. *Serviceability*. Another type of concern that consumers often have is how long it will take to repair a product if it breaks down. For example, most consumers want to know that if their furnace breaks down, it will be repaired within a day or less.

7. *Aesthetics*. The seventh dimension is how a product looks, feels, sounds, tastes, or smells. Here, there is no universal standard. On the other hand, anyone who has helped to build a clubhouse for

children knows that even at an early age strong preferences for design, color, shape, and functionality enter into the evaluation of the final product.

8. *Perceived quality*. Reputation is often the basis for perceived quality, and the quality of previous products is often used as the basis to predict future performance. Thus, firms like Maytag can introduce new products and safely boast about their reliability because many consumers have already experienced this from other product purchases.

If these eight dimensions can be used to build a quality strategy, can they also be used to detect strategic errors? The answer is yes. As Garvin (1987) noted, these errors typically fall into two camps. One error is to incorporate a quality dimension(s) that consumers really don't care about. A good test here is the willingness of a customer to pay for an additional characteristic. If everyone wants it, but no one is willing to pay for it, then don't include it. The other common error is to fail to respond to a dimension that is, in fact, really important to customers. This error can often be traced back to weak market research that fails to reveal what consumers really value in a product or service. When this happens, much to the chagrin of a firm's management, feedback about this error may come only in the form of reduced sales and profits.

Robust Quality

While early work on quality improvement stressed the importance of reducing defects in the production process, later writers like Taguchi and Clausing (1990) challenged this whole approach by emphasizing that the real test of a product's quality is not how it leaves the factory but, rather, only how it works in the field. In other words, to exceed customers' expectations, it is essential to have a product work in ways or under conditions that even the customers did not imagine when they asked for the product. Hitting this higher standard of quality has been nicely captured in the term "robust quality."

Advocates of this approach to quality management ground their position on the economic reality that failures in the field are much more expensive than failures in the factory. Specifically, when a product fails in the field, it will cost a firm more than just the price of production. The company will also incur costs associated with warranties, rework, shipping, and, ultimately, a loss of reputation. Writers from this perspective call these expenses the loss quality function (LQF), which, according to their view, rises exponentially as problems are detected farther out from the factory floor.

To avoid these expensive experiences Taguchi and Clausing (1990), in particular, have offered a number of ideas for rethinking how to improve quality and methods to be put into place in an organization to make these ideas part of a firm's overall quality strategy. Their first recommendation is to start by recognizing that quality is, first and foremost, a virtue of good design. Indeed, in their view the value of a good design can swamp the return on investment for any efforts aimed at trying to control the production process itself. Second, they suggest that efforts aimed at obtaining zero defects in the production process are just wrong-headed. This strident view is based on the observation that zero defects can still lead to imperfect products down the line (i.e., due to tolerance stack-up), and imperfect products lead to angry customers. Instead, they argue that the best way to decrease defects in the production process is by creating a better product design that will work robustly in the field.

The heart of their argument is based on statistical analysis. In particular, they call into question the value of statistical process control because it can lead to a false sense of security. For instance, a production manager can be pleased that all of his or her products are within specification. Yet, according to the authors, the fundamental concern in production should not be about making something that falls within an acceptable range of tolerance. Rather, the goal should be to deliver a product that is consistently on "target." That is, a consistent product, whether or not it is within a specified range, is better than a product that always falls within a band of acceptable variation because in the former case simple adjustments can make consistent products work. In contrast, when greater variability is present, albeit still within an acceptable range of tolerance, many variables will need to be explored to bring the product into alignment.

A more desirable approach to quality management, therefore, is to begin by understanding how customers will actually use the product in the field. Working from this perspective, the key is to identify up front all of the variables (e.g., heat, humidity, mishandling) that will affect its use. Once these key variables are identified, then experiments can be conducted to see how changes in the key variables will interact to determine the product's ultimate performance. Given this information, a prototype can be created and compared against the current benchmark product in a system verification test (SVT). Prototypes continue to be built until they can outperform the current best product. Once this happens, the prototype can go into production with less attention being paid to ensuring that it is within shop floor specifications because the designers and producers know that it will work in the field.

QUALITY STANDARD 3: DELIGHTING CUSTOMERS

If exceeding customer expectations is a commendable goal, better still is the ability to win the loyalty of customers by delighting them. Generating loyalty can be critical to the financial success of firms for two related economic reasons. First, research has consistently shown that when managed correctly, loyal customers are more profitable customers because, at a minimum, as relationships lengthen, transaction costs can decrease for both parties. This simple economic reality is a function of the fact that parties to long-term relationships come to learn how each other's systems work, and over time they can simplify how they work together. The other key factor driving profitability is that loyal customers talk to others, and good words win referrals. Given these facts of economic life, a more recent goal of quality improvement has become to delight customers. Following are insights into how some firms are pursuing this quality goal.

Zero Defections

Much of the early work on quality improvement was centered on the manufacturing sector. Concepts like zero defects and robust quality make sense there. In the service sector, however, these ideas have often had a hollow ring. On the other hand, during the 1990s firms in this sector have been able to readily understand the idea that to win a customer's loyalty, you need to create a delightful experience (Pine and Gilmore, 1998), which will lead to zero defections (Reichheld and Sasser, 1990).

It must be emphasized here that pursuing zero defections is more than just a phrase. In the service sector it has been shown to be a powerful strategic concept. Indeed, studies have shown that by retaining just 5% more of its current customers, a firm's profits can increase almost 100% (Reichheld and Sasser, 1990). To be successful in this quality strategy, though, a few basic things must be done very well. For example, companies must begin to watch their door very carefully. That is, it is critical to monitor the flow of business coming from a customer. Retail businesses such as restaurants, clothing shops, and movie rental companies have done this with relative ease by making use of credit cards to track the ebb and flow of purchases. With this information, they have built profiles of customer purchasing patterns and then tailored advertisements to individuals and businesses based on their unique pattern of buying decisions. Second, firms also need to take quick action when it appears that their volume of business is declining. This is often a signal that a defection is forthcoming. Polite calls to soon-to-be defectors can give the organization invaluable insights into what is happening within their market. Third, listening posts need to be set up. This can be easily done by monitoring customer service calls and complaints.

What all these tactics have in common is a determination on the part of the firm to proactively answer several important, strategic questions that have everything to do with making current and future quality decisions. First, using these techniques, firms can discover how customers learn about the availability of goods and services. Second, they can track the popularity of specific offerings over time and then follow up to discover the reason(s) (e.g., price competition, items going out of fashion) that sales are increasing or decreasing. Third, when customers leave, it is possible to find out where are they going and for what reason.

Armed with this rich information, it becomes possible to determine more precisely what type of customers is best for the firm given its current internal capabilities, and, equally important, what type of customers will not be pursued going forward. This last point is very important and is addressed in more detail in Chapter 5. Specifically, to meet higher-quality standards, firms must become more disciplined in determining whom they will and will not serve. When you aim to delight some customers, it means that others will not be served.

Meaning of Quality in the Information Age

From the preceding discussion it is clear that the definition of quality has been changing over time and across sectors of the economy. For example, in the manufacturing arena, where most of the original passion for improving quality first gained a foothold, the initial quality standard of conformance to specifications evolved into the pursuit of zero defects and now on to robust quality. At the same time, firms in the service sector have come to realize that using manufacturing measures of excellence just do not work in their world. Rather, quality goals such as zero defections based on creating a special experience for a select group of customers make more sense. As we move into the information age, a whole new set of issues around how to define quality is emerging. Specifically, in this arena, quality may well have more to do with the capacity of a firm to provide a portfolio approach to defining quality that encompasses a number of different definitions depending on the software application being used and the skills and the needs of users of the system.

More precisely, as Prahalad and Krishnan (1999) have recently noted, in the information age the new nerve center of a growing number of firms is their software. Indeed, the quality of experiences enjoyed by customers, employees, suppliers, and even investors may be determined significantly by the software in use within a firm. Yet, in confronting this emerging reality, there are good news and bad news. The good news is that the capacity of information technology (IT) to handle ever more complex problems is growing exponentially every day. The bad news is that many of these systems do not work together very well or at all.

Working together, moreover, is also not as simple as it might sound because to have a really high-quality IT support system, often at least three different quality definitions need to be blended together within a firm. Specifically, depending on the application and the end-users, a top-end system must provide *conformance to specifications, service,* and the *capacity to experiment and innovate.* This is because a software application domain has three primary characteristics (i.e., specificity, stability, and evolvability), which are more or less important depending on what it is designed to do. For example, financial systems need to be specific and conform to a widely agreed upon set of rules. On the other hand, systems that may be accessed by users with widely varying information needs and levels of skill in navigating a system must provide a user-friendly service interface. At the same time, systems such as e-commerce must constantly evolve.

Obviously, managing all these needs is an enormous task, and so, perhaps not surprisingly, the potential returns from the vast storehouses of information being created are not being equally realized. Certainly, firms like Wal-Mart, Dell Computers, Eastman Chemicals, and Amazon.com are flourishing in this new information-rich environment. On the other hand, major firms such as General Motors are laboring hard to get over 7,800 distinct software systems to work together (Prahalad and Krishnan, 1999). Clearly, the price to be paid for being considered a true quality player in the information age is great, but so, too, are the rewards for those who succeed.

CREATING NEW POSSIBILITIES

Throughout this chapter we have emphasized how quality standards are constantly evolving and the critical role that process improvement can play in aiding firms to remain competitive in light of rapidly changing market conditions. Since our primary concern is with how to build a quality organization, however, it is fitting to conclude by asking what happens to a firm when the decision is made to become a truly process-oriented organization. The simple answer is that this decision usually creates a wealth of new possibilities for the firm, but at the same time management must fundamentally rethink how it does business, and frankly this can be traumatic.

The reason for this good news—bad news scenario is that while all firms have processes, most were never structured around processes, nor do they have a culture that rewards organization-wide process improvement efforts (Byrne, 1993). Therefore, despite all the knowledge developed over the last several decades on how to make the transition to a process oriented style of management, only a relatively few organizations have actually made the full transition.

There are several fundamental and interrelated reasons for this lack of movement. Certainly, part of the reason for this lack of movement has been technical and structural in nature. That is, prior to relatively recent advances in information technology, the most effective way to move information in most firms was, in fact, by utilizing a management system known as command and control. This system, which traces its origins to the birth of the Roman empire and the Roman Catholic Church, has well-developed technical methods for transferring large volumes of information, and they work rather well in fairly stable environments. On the other hand, command and control structures also emphasize functional and hierarchical reporting relationships at the expense of cross-functional collaboration, and these forces in combination tend to foster and reward "silo" cultures. That is, rewards go to those who take care of their departments and themselves first and the organization-as-a-whole second.

Accordingly, after command and control structures and cultures have been in place for a while, they become extremely difficult to change because most employees know the rules of the game, and the best players have been rewarded and promoted for their abilities to effectively work the system. Thus, while leaders may envision a better future by moving from a command and control world to a process-oriented organization, the resistance to doing so can be deep and multifaceted (Fairfield-Sonn,

1993). Only the determined and courageous will be able to simultaneously attack and tear down the old system and replace it with a new one. Moreover, success may well be determined as much by the leaders' will to execute as by their knowledge about how to execute (Charan and Colvin, 1999).

Clearly, the decision to become a process-oriented organization will not be made lightly or even entered into willingly by everyone. Yet, several leading-edge firms including SmithKline Beecham, Xerox, Pepsi, and United Services Automobile Association (USAA) have all done it. Why did they decide to do it? Each had its own unique reasons for doing so. However, as the reader will soon see, they had a common driver; namely, in every instance the business case was so compelling and the cost of not doing it sufficiently large that making the move became the most prudent course of action (Garvin, 1995).

For example, according to Jan Leschly, chief executive of SmithKline Beecham, the decision to become process-oriented came after its whole customer base suddenly changed. Historically, this pharmaceutical firm had been physician-driven. When changes in the medical delivery system swept across the United States and Europe, however, it awoke to discover that its new customers were employers, insurance companies in the United States, and governments in Europe. To make matters worse, it knew very little about any of them. After some serious soul-searching, it concluded that it could no longer run four separate silo businesses in pharmaceuticals, consumer health care, animal health, and clinical laboratories and hope to continue in business. Further analysis led it to decide to move forward by creating new strategies for, and focusing on, three key, cross-functional, process-oriented businesses, namely, care delivery, care management, and care coverage (Garvin, 1995).

At Xerox, Paul Allaire, chairman and CEO, and his senior team decided to become a process-oriented firm for much the same reason as SmithKline Beecham. An in-depth analysis of the future of their business in 1989 led them to conclude that their customers' needs and requirements would be dramatically different going forward. To meet these new needs, they would have to shed their focus on manufacturing copiers, printers, and facsimile products and instead begin providing document tools and services to help their clients meet their productivity needs. Thus, a new strategy, a new structure, and a new identity as the Document Company were born (Garvin, 1995).

The crisis, if you will, for Craig Weatherup, president and CEO of Pepsi, came in the late 1980s from an internal decision. At that time the firm made a $4 billion bet that the future would be brighter if they bought up their bottling distribution network. As Pepsi soon discovered, however, buying the network was easy compared to trying to operate it, for a simple reason. In purchasing the network, the firm quickly moved from the need to serve 600 customers to having to work effectively with 600,000 customers. Meanwhile, it also decided that even with this significant shift in its business, it wanted to retain its distinctive style of big promotion marketing. It soon discovered that to have both parts work in harmony, it would be critical to significantly improve internal operations. After reflecting on the challenges for the future, it concluded that only a shift to organization-wide process management systems would allow this to happen (Garvin, 1995).

Finally, for Robert Herres, chairman and CEO of USAA, the impetus to become truly process-oriented came from the experience of dealing with mounting pains due to growth, the concomitant pressures of having customers complain that no one in the organization seemed to speak to each other anymore, and the realization that advances in information technology might allow the firm to rethink how it did business. As a result, the senior management team concluded that only by becoming more process-oriented could it continue to provide the level of service that was acceptable to its customer population (Garvin, 1995).

In conclusion, the intent of this chapter has been two-fold. First, an effort was made to explain how and why quality standards have and will continue to evolve over time. Specifically, companies' and consumers' quality standards result from the interaction of the capacity of firms within an industry to produce goods and services at varying levels of quality, market conditions, and the influence of interested third parties.

The other intent was to make clear that becoming a quality organization is a matter of choice. Every organization must decide for itself how much quality is appropriate to be successful.

No universal standard exists. Regardless of what standard is selected, however, the leaders of the firm must think hard about what this decision will mean for their customers, employees, investors, and themselves (Zeithaml, 1988). As the review of several prominent thinkers on how to improve quality revealed, there are many ways to move forward on this agenda, but all demand the willingness and flexibility to adopt new strategies, new structures, and, most importantly, a new culture to support these adjustments as customer needs and requirements change. Becoming a quality-driven company is not an easy task, but the rewards will be commensurate with the investment.

REFERENCES

Aguayo, R. 1990. *Dr. Deming: The American who taught the Japanese about quality*. New York: Simon & Schuster.

Buzzell, R. D., & Gale, B. T. 1987. *The PIMS (profit impact of market strategy) principles: Linking strategy to performance*. New York: Free Press.

Byrne, J. A. 1993. The horizontal corporation. *Business Week*, December 20: 77–81.

Carsky, M. L., Dickinson, R. A. & Canedy, C. R. III. 1998. The evolution of quality in consumer goods. *Journal of Macromarketing*, 18 (2): 132–143.

Charan, R., & Colvin, G. 1999. Why CEOs fail. *Fortune*, 139 (12): 68–72, 74, 76, 78.

Crosby, P. B. 1988. *The eternally successful organization: The art of corporate wellness*. New York: McGraw-Hill.

Crosby, P. B. 1979. *Quality is free: The art of making quality certain*. New York: McGraw-Hill.

Deming, W. E. 1986. *Out of the crisis*. Cambridge: MIT Center for Advanced Engineering Study.

Deming, W. E. 1982. *Quality, productivity, and competitive position*. Cambridge: MIT Center of Advanced Engineering Study.

Fairfield-Sonn, J.W. 1999. Influence of context on process improvement teams: Leadership from a distance. *Journal of Business and Economic Studies*, 5 (2): 61–80.

Fairfield-Sonn, J. W. 1993. Moving beyond vision: Fostering cultural change in a bureaucracy. *Journal of Organizational Change Management*, 6 (5): 43–55.

Fairfield-Sonn, J. W., & Lacey, N. 1996. Prospects for small business in Poland's future. *Managerial Finance*, 22 (10): 64–72.

Gale, B. T. 1994. *Managing customer value*. New York: Free Press.

Garvin, D. A. 1995. Leveraging processes for strategic advantage: A roundtable with Xerox's Allaire, USAA's Herres, SmithKline Beecham's Leschly, and Pepsi's Weatherup. *Harvard Business Review*, 73 (5): 76–90.

Garvin, D. A. 1987. Competing on the eight dimensions of quality. *Harvard Business Review*, 65 (6): 101–109.

Hamel, G. & Prahalad, C.K. 1994. Competing for the future. *Harvard Business Review*, 72 (4): 122–128.

Juran, J. M. 1988. *Juran on planning for quality*. New York: Free Press.

Kotler, P., Jatusripitak, S., & Maesincee, S. 1997. *The marketing of nations*. New York: Free Press.

March, A., & Garvin, D. A. 1986. A note on quality: The views of Deming, Juran, and Crosby 17–29. Boston: Harvard Business School Publishing.

Nader, R. 1966. *Unsafe at any speed*. New York: Pocket Books.

Pine, J. B. II, & Gilmore, J. H. 1998. Welcome to the experience economy. *Harvard Business Review*, 76 (4): 97–105.

Prahalad, C. K., & Krishnan, M. S. 1999. The new meaning of quality in the information age. *Harvard Business Review*, 77 (5): 109–118.

Reichheld, F. F., & Sasser, W. E., Jr. 1990. Zero defections: Quality comes to services. *Harvard Business Review*, 68 (5): 105–111.

Sinclair, U. 1906. *The jungle*. New York: New American Library.

Taguchi, G., & Clausing, D. 1990. Robust quality. *Harvard Business Review*, 68 (1): 65–75.

Zeithaml, V. 1988. Consumer perceptions of price, quality, and value: A means-end model and synthesis of evidence. *Journal of Marketing*, 52 (7): 2–22.

Chapter 2

Creating a Quality Culture

Excellence is a habit.

—Aristotle

As individuals, we are all creatures of habits. Our habits are often so pervasive, subtle, and deeply rooted that they go unnoticed by us unless questioned or commented upon by someone else. Nonetheless, they have a profound impact on the way we get through each day. In the same way, organizations are creatures of habits. Every organization develops its own way of working over time. We call this way of doing everyday business a corporate culture. Fortunately, for us as individuals and organizations as a whole, when necessary, habits can be changed. Changing habits may not be easy or fun, but if the rewards are sufficiently great, then the effort will be worth it. In this chapter, the focus is on understanding how corporate cultures form and change over time with an eye toward understanding how an organization can make continuous quality improvement a central part of the way it does business.

WHAT IS CORPORATE CULTURE?

Many definitions of corporate culture have been offered over the years. The simplest definition, noted earlier, is merely "how we do business here." Yet, the how in this statement masks a complex, multifaceted, collective knowledge of lessons learned and values to be honored that are not always easily recognized or appreciated by casual observers. Rather, corporate culture has been appropriately likened to a volcano in the sense that it contains many layers that you must work through to get to the fiery core. To understand the deeper nature of a firm's culture, therefore, it is necessary to expand your understanding of each of these layers (Schein, 1985; Fairfield-Sonn, 1984).

The reward for this effort is to emerge from the journey with a deeper appreciation for what the organization really values (e.g., maximizing short-term profits, creating new, innovative products, etc.). To help you visualize how these layers are related, Figure 2.1 depicts a four-layer model of corporate culture, followed by a brief description of the contents of each layer.

Cultural Artifacts

Continuing with the metaphor, on the surface of the volcano we encounter the cooled "cultural artifacts" of an organization. These artifacts, such as the company's physical facilities, formal policies about promotion requirements, hours of work, and so on, and official documents such as the organization chart can give some clues about what a firm might value, but they need to be taken with a grain of salt.

For example, it takes only a quick visual inspection of a typical defense contractor's plant to guess that life inside the walls will be fairly regimented. In contrast, the more elegant offices preferred by the major accounting firms would suggest that working there would be a very different experience. Yet, in reality, there is wide variation among the cultures of both defense contracting firms and accounting firms. For example, when Price Waterhouse recently merged with Coopers and Lybrand, the *Wall Street Journal* questioned how well the cultures of the two firms might blend since, as they summarized it, the Price Water-house folks like to wear starched underwear, and the folks at Coopers and Lybrand don't like to wear any underwear.

Figure 2.1
Four Levels of Corporate Culture

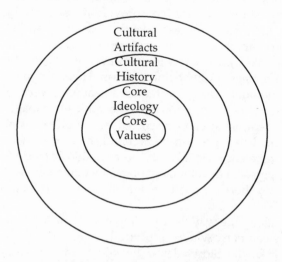

The preceding comment should not be interpreted to mean that one culture is better than another. Cultures, particularly strong ones with well-understood and widely shared values, are just different. However, these differences carry with them important consequences that must be taken seriously by anyone making a decision about whether or not to work for a firm.

Cultural History

Going below the surface level of culture, the next level has been described as the "cultural history" (Fairfield-Sonn, 1984). Any organization that has been in operation for over a year will have at least the beginning of a cultural history, and older, more successful firms often have a very rich cultural history. Exploring this level of culture can be very rewarding because it contains insights rarely gleaned from even the most thorough review of the official handbook of policies and procedures. In other words, there is official policy, and then there is a collective internal memory, captured in *stories*, of what is truly rewarded and punished in the firm (Neuhauser, 1993).

Some of these stories are essentially about how best to get through each workday, while others can be about organizational *heroines* and *heroes*. In every case they provide deeper insights into how the business really works. Take the case of a new employee who is very ambitious. In his employment interview with the company, he takes great pains to learn everything possible about what it takes to get promoted in the firm. He is pleased to learn that the promotion process in the organization is very orderly. For example, to get promoted to the rank of manager, there are seven identifiable tasks discussed in the official company policy manual that need to be accomplished at a clearly stated level of competence. He takes this information as true and starts to create a personal development plan aimed at meeting all seven criteria in as short a period of time as possible (Morgan and Dennehy, 1997).

Fortunately, along the way, he runs into one of the longtime employees of the company who is respectfully referred to as the Storyteller. He asks the Storyteller if he knows of any cases where someone has met all the seven criteria and still not received a promotion. Oh, yes, replies the Storyteller, and the new employee learns that while the seven criteria are important to meet, there are also some things that he should never do if he hopes to get promoted. The new employee's education continues when he further asks the Storyteller if he knows of anyone who did not meet all of the criteria and was promoted out of cycle. Once again, the Storyteller smiles and shares with the youth some things that are very beneficial to do that never appear on the official list. This information is greatly appreciated by the new employee and will prove invaluable to him in his quest for the promotion.

Rites and rituals are also an important part of the cultural history of the firm. These events are rarely random, and, particularly when they are led by senior members of the organization, they may well have symbolic value that far exceeds their surface importance. For example, a talented woman who had been a visiting nurse for 12 years decided that she wanted to work for a major metropolitan hospital as part of her personal development plan. She applied for a job and was accepted. During the first few months on the job everything went very well.

Then it happened. The hospital was holding its annual pin ceremony for nurses who had been at the hospital for 5, 10, or more years. Not recognizing the cultural importance of the event, she arrived a little late and slipped into a chair at the back of the large auditorium, which was almost filled to capacity.

After the hospital president completed his general remarks, he began calling off the names of the nurses who would receive their five-year pins. As the recipients started moving toward the podium, she noticed that the nurses were all starting to cry. This new nurse could not understand the reason for the tears, and so she started to laugh. After a few chuckles, however, the entire audience became silent, and then everyone turned to look at her. Slinking down deep into her chair, she knew that something was very wrong.

Only after the meeting, when she was curtly informed that the average tenure of the nurses in this hospital was 9 months and that the nurses receiving the pins were therefore viewed as the heroines of the hospital did she realize what she had done. By laughing at the cultural heroines of the organization she had unknowingly committed career suicide in the hospital. She would never be forgiven for this cultural violation. Shortly thereafter, she began polishing up her résumé and left the hospital to return to the field.

Symbols can also play an important role in explaining the essence of a culture and maintaining certain values over time. Sometimes a symbol can be a word. For instance, THINK is an important symbol at IBM, as it reflects the serious nature of the analytical work that needs to be accomplished to be successful in the very competitive computer industry. At other times, an individual or a group of individuals can become a symbol for an organization. Certainly, the original group of National Aeronautical and Space Administration (NASA) astronauts came to represent the determination of the American space program to beat the Russians in the race to conquer space.

Language likewise plays an important role in transmitting cultural values. Creating a code language is particularly important because it allows organizational members to refer to highly sought after goals or distasteful situations in a more neutral way. For example, the term "high potential" has often been used to describe someone who has been chosen to have accelerated career advancement opportunities. On the other hand, the term reduction in forces (RIF) has been used to describe the need to endure another round of layoffs. Almost every organization will develop internal code words to describe complex situations that have led to positive or negative results for the organization. As individuals are socialized into the culture of the organization, these words or phrases can prove to be invaluable guides to how they should conduct themselves when similar situations arise.

Core Ideology

Below the cultural history lies the organization's core ideology. Not many firms articulate their ideology very well, but when they do, these statements become highly informative and often sacred. Johnson & Johnson's credo is a good example. This document, which is widely distributed inside and outside the organization, clearly identifies the cultural imperatives of the company, in order of priority, that guide decision making within the firm. The credo begins with this clear statement: "We believe our first responsibility is to the doctors, nurses and patients, to mothers and all others who use our products and services. In meeting their needs everything we do must be of high quality." Indeed, this credo is so central to how decisions are made in the company that when several individuals died in Chicago due to tampering with bottles of Tylenol, then CEO, Burke, reported that he largely made a $600 million decision within 48 hours to remove every bottle of the drug from every shelf in the world after reflecting on what the company said that it stood for in its credo.

Core Values

Finally, at the deepest level of culture are the core values of the organization. Often, these values are known only to the innermost circle of decision makers within a firm. Sometimes these values are explicitly discussed within the group. At other times, they are so deeply held that they become undiscussable. In either case, core values are nonetheless powerful guides to how decisions will be made today and in the future because they are just the way that a "good" business should be run.

For example, in one family-owned business a core value was that the firm must always be controlled by the male blood relatives. As a result, the business was divided in such a way that each male partner had his own region to run. Not surprisingly, opportunities to expand the business were always ultimately decided on the basis of whether or not there was a new male relative in need of a position. Thus, when a young male blood relative needed a position, the company would move into a new territory. In the absence of this need, any number of convenient reasons would be offered to explain why expansion would not be prudent at that time.

WHY CULTURE MATTERS

There are many ways to measure organizational success. In the first chapter, we discussed how creating a continuous improvement work culture can lead to the capacity to create higher-quality products and services. This capacity, in turn, can lead to greater profitability.

There is evidence to suggest that culture also plays a central role in another important measure of success, namely, longevity. The strongest support for this contention comes from a recent study by de Geus (1997), who was interested in discovering the answer to three important management questions. First, as a practical matter, how long can a corporation live? Second, what is the average life span of corporations? Third, in what ways are long-lived corporations different from those with shorter life spans?

In answer to the first two questions, de Geus found that one Swedish firm called Stora, currently a major producer of paper, pulp, and chemicals, has been in operation for over 700 years. Thus, it seems that firms could potentially exist for a very long time. However, when we learn, as de Geus discovered, that the average life expectancy of all the firms in his study was less than 50 years, it raises some serious questions about what is happening to limit the life span of so many firms.

What explains the tremendous early mortality rate among most firms? As de Geus looked carefully at 27 very successful organizations, such as DuPont, W.R. Grace, Sumitomo, and Siemens, that have existed for over 100 years, he found an important common pattern. Specifically, unlike the vast majority of firms that primarily pursue economic gains in a particular industry, all of these long-lived firms placed a greater value on creating a community of individuals who know, as members of the firm, who they are and why they hold certain values in common. That is, all of the long-lived firms had nurtured and treasured a strong corporate culture that served them well over time.

Indeed, during their existence, all of the firms in de Geus' study had moved at least once into a totally new line of business. Yet, while the focus of their business activities changed, their core values remained intact. The four most common values were to be conservative in financing, so they could take advantage of opportunities that presented themselves at different times; to be sensitive to the world around them, so they could learn and adapt to changes in the marketplace; to be aware of their identity, in the sense that, no matter how broadly they diversified their business, employees still felt that they were integral parts of a whole; and to be tolerant of new ideas that might lead to the next successful phase in their growth and development. Thus, while the business environment around them changed, their core values provided a sense of stability and purpose that allowed them to successfully adapt to ever evolving demands.

In summary, why does corporate culture help to explain varying levels of profitability and longevity? The answer lies in the fact that culture impacts organizational performance, team performance, and individual performance. The performance connection stems directly from the fact that cultural norms and values affect "how" everyday decisions are made about the way work gets done. In this sense, culture is a pervasive influence that touches everyone in every organization in a myriad of big and small ways every day.

Organizational Performance

More precisely, on the organizational level, anecdotal evidence about the connection between culture and performance has been available for a very long time. In the early 1980s, however, more systematic evidence started to mount with the publication of two influential books on the subject.

One of these books, which quickly became one of the best-selling books of all time, was called *In Search of Excellence* (Peters and Waterman, 1982). The authors' intent in writing this book was to identify those factors that were most useful in explaining why a select group of large firms drawn from the fields of high technology, consumer goods, manufacturing, service, project management, and resource-based production had been able to enjoy substantial growth and profitability over a 20-year time span.

In looking carefully at 43 major firms, the authors distilled eight consistent, although not universally present, characteristics that helped collectively to explain the performance of these firms. These habits were a bias for taking action rather than overanalyzing issues; a drive to get close to customers; the willingness to grant employees sufficient autonomy such that they could explore new entrepreneurial activities; seeking to improve productivity by investing in their people; hands-on, value-driven styles of management; a preference for sticking to businesses that they knew how to run; creating simple structures and operating with a lean staff; and granting operational autonomy at the shop floor while retaining centralized control over the values of the firm writ large.

Yet, the authors found that more than just a specific set of values set these firms apart from their less successful rivals; the intensity with which these values were embraced in these firms seemed to explain their power to positively affect performance.

That is, the values of these firms had become so deeply embedded in the habits of the firm that, regardless of what external challenges surfaced, the employees knew just how they had to handle them.

The other major influential book published in the early 1980s was *Corporate Cultures* (Deal and Kennedy, 1982). This book, which is credited with first popularizing the term "corporate culture," took a slightly different approach to the subject. These authors, like Peters and Waterman, began by selecting a group of solid firms to study. In their case, the initial population numbered 80. Then, they conducted in-depth interviews with representatives from these firms to determine if they held any clearly articulated beliefs and, if so, what they were. What they discovered was that only about one-third of the firms had any widely held consensus about their core beliefs. Drilling down another level, they discovered that roughly two-thirds of the firms with strong beliefs had qualitative beliefs such as "IBM means service." The other third had financial goals that were widely shared.

When they analyzed the performance of their sample of firms, they were struck by the fact that all 18 firms with strong qualitative beliefs, that is, firms with strong, well-articulated cultures, had enjoyed outstanding performance for a long time. In contrast, they could not find any similar factor to explain the performance of the other firms. Some of the comparison firms had done well, some had just gotten by, and others had their ups and downs. Given this data, they concluded that having a strong culture should be viewed as a significant asset for a firm to possess (Raspa, 1990).

Unlike Peters and Waterman, however, these researchers were not content just to report this important culture- performance relationship. Rather, they wanted to know how strong cultures were formed and how they were being sustained over time. Their search led them to discover that some specific, identifiable methods for creating and carrying on cultural traditions did, in fact, exist. For example, within these strong culture companies, there were frequently living or past heroes, such as Buck Rogers at IBM or Thomas Edison at General Electric, who served as role models for how to live the company's values. Likewise, there were often rites or rituals ranging from the Friday afternoon "beer bust" at Tandem, to the annual Mary Kay gala celebration that helped to clarify and institutionalize the values. Moreover, on a day-to-day basis, there were rich communication networks at work, led by those functioning as storytellers, priests, and gossips, who served to carry on the message of the importance of preserving the firm's cultural heritage.

Another contribution that the researchers made to our understanding of the impact of corporate culture on life within firms was that while every firm has a unique culture, there appeared to be sufficient evidence to suggest that there are also what they called "cultural tribes." Moreover, each of these tribes had habitual ways of working that made it successful within specific work environments.

Deal and Kennedy identified and described four of these tribes as follows. One tribe was called the tough-guy, macho culture where rugged individualists routinely take high risks and get quick feedback on whether they are right or wrong. Police departments, surgeons, and entertainers of all sorts live and thrive in this world. Another distinctive culture is devoted to hard work and hard play. Fun and action are the drivers here, where employees maintain high levels of relatively low-risk activity. Notable examples here are sales-driven organizations ranging from automotive distributors to the likes of Frito-Lay and Xerox. The third tribe embraces a bet-your-company culture where big stakes decisions are made, and it may take years to see how the deal turns out. Oil companies like Exxon fit this profile, as they place huge bets that new wells will lead to significant new resource discoveries. Finally, there are process cultures, where employees get relatively little feedback on how well they are doing at any time, so they learn to trust that how they get their work done will eventually lead to a positive result. Government agencies, insurance companies, and utilities often fall into this category.

In the wake of these two books, a whole industry of culture change experts was spawned aimed primarily at helping firms to develop stronger corporate cultures (*Inc.*, 1999). During the next decade, many tools and techniques were developed to help bring about a cultural transformation, particularly in firms less successful than those chronicled in the two groundbreaking books. The results of this effort, however, were mixed. In some firms substantial progress was made, while in others little changed. Worse yet, some firms that aggressively developed stronger cultures fell on hard financial times. It seemed that the hope of finding business salvation through cultural change was proving to be as elusive as Ponce de Leon's search for the fountain of eternal youth.

In 1992, however, at least part of the mystery behind why culture change efforts were not universally successful was solved with the publication of another significant study on the relationship between corporate culture and organizational performance. Specifically, in a comprehensive study of over 200 firms, Kotter and Heskett (1992) found that firms with strong cultures that were *adaptable* and *changed with the times* were successful over time. On the other hand, firms with strong cultures that led them to become complacent or arrogant were as likely to fall on bad times as firms with weak cultures.

A few years later, Collins and Porras (1994) provided even more insight into the profound, long-term influence that corporate culture can have on performance when they published their study of a select group of firms with a most enviable track record. Collectively, the companies in their report had outperformed the general stock market by a factor of 15 for over five decades.

What did these firms have in common? In every case they had a shared culture that ran deeply throughout the organization. That is, foreshadowing the study by de Geus, all these firms had a central set of corporate values that had remained intact since their very beginning. Moreover, several of the firms in their study had not only changed the focus of the businesses but were doing business in totally different industries.

For example, one of their exemplar companies, Minnesota Mining & Manufacturing (3M), had begun as a mining company but had evolved into a diversified abrasives and adhesives company. Throughout this major transition, however, it never lost sight of the fact that its core reason for being was "to solve unsolved problems innovatively." Thus, by remaining true to its strongest core value, the company was able to move into new industries because it could still continue to be true to their central purpose. What lesson did Collins and Porras draw from observing these successful, long-lived firms in action? Their simple, yet compelling, conclusion was that each of these firms had been able to thrive over a very long time and even in new markets because it had simultaneously maintained continuity in its core values while being open to changing everything else.

Team Performance

Culture's influence on performance, however, is seen not only on the organizational level. It also impacts team performance. Specifically, with the growing use of teams to achieve a wide variety of organizational objectives (Mohrman, Cohen, and Mohrman, 1995) there has been a mounting interest in learning why some groups work, and others don't (Hackman, 1990). To this point, it is useful to know that research has revealed that high-performing teams actually exhibit remarkably similar cultural norms around how to do their work, regardless of the type of organization that they are in (Katzenbach and Smith, 1993). Foremost among these characteristics are the development of shared goals, mutual accountability for results, clearly defined roles and responsibilities based on maximizing each individual's strengths, and shared leadership.

Individual Performance

Finally, corporate culture also impacts individual performance in two important ways. One way that performance is impacted stems from the need for employees and employers to come to a mutual understanding of what constitutes a "good way" to do a job as well as what needs to be done. When there is agreement on these two important issues, the relationship typically works well. On the other hand, particularly when strong differences emerge around the "how to" issue, tensions will invariably mount for both parties. Even when the results are good, management will still be disappointed. Meanwhile, employees will be frustrated by the constant pressure to change how they do their work.

Another source of pressure stemming from cultural value conflicts between an organization and an individual can come from finding meaning in one's work. For example, an individual who believes in the values of promoting good health may find it easy to work for a pharmaceutical company. On the other hand, if an individual works for one of the successful, popular soda companies but views the job as just manufacturing sweetened, brown, carbonated water, he or she may have great difficulty in remaining enthusiastic about promoting the firm's products, and, over the long term, individual performance will suffer.

CHANGING CORPORATE CULTURE

Considerable debate has raged over the last two decades around whether or not corporate culture can or should be consciously changed. In fact, every organization has its own unique culture that is constantly evolving (Peters and Waterman, 1982; Deal and Kennedy, 1982). This reality is captured graphically in Figure 2.2. The question that management must answer, therefore, is how actively involved it should become in shaping and managing the culture (Kilmann, 1989; Schein, 1985; Davis, 1984). Naturally, this includes a consideration of the degree to which quality improvement is or will become a central part of the organization's value system (Baldrige National Quality Program, 2000).

More precisely, as Figure 2.2 shows, corporate culture exists in a state of constant flux. When a new organization is created, leaders typically focus on creating a vision for what the organization is to become. At the same time, whether or not conscious decisions are made about it, a culture will start to "emerge" out of the day-to-day necessity to define how work will get done. Some of these decisions about how to do the work will be the result of deliberate, obvious choices. Meanwhile, other decisions will come about through trial-and-error experimentation based on intuitive hunches about the best way to handle business problems. These hunches themselves are derived from deeply held core values. Regardless of how they are made, over time, the most beneficial decisions about how to handle organizational issues will start to take on more permanence. Eventually, some of these will take on the power of "established" cultural norms, and, as long as they work reasonably well, they will remain, for the most part, unchallenged.

Figure 2.2
Changing Patterns of Consensus about Work Values

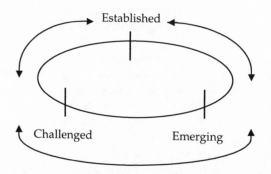

Over time, however, every organization will ultimately face new issues where older, tried-and-true strategies just do not work. When this happens, prevailing cultural norms may and should be "challenged." As alternative ways of addressing these issues are sought, it may be found that other, more effective ways to handle them exist. Thus, new business paradigms will emerge, and they, in turn, will hold sway until they likewise are challenged and replaced. In this sense, cultural norms are always present and always subject to change.

The recent boom in merger and acquisition activity, in particular, has created many high-profile situations (Bauman, Jackson, and Lawrence, 1997) that show how the model in Figure 2.2 can provide some useful insights into the impact of culture on organizational life (Buono and Bowditch, 1989). For instance, in the case of mergers of relative equals, what we often see is a collision of well-established cultures that leads to many culture-related performance concerns. After the marriage has been consummated, and the two firms begin to try to work together, it quickly becomes apparent that there are, in fact, good, rival ways of attacking many common problems. To resolve the resulting challenges to cultural norms, the firms need to come to some sort of an agreement about which of the current ways or what new norms for doing the work of the firm should be established as they move forward (Weber, 1996). In the case of an acquisition, a somewhat different, yet equally powerful dynamic is often experienced. Here, it is usually the acquired firm that feels the full force of a cultural collision on a firm as members of the acquired firm quickly learn that they must change the way that they have traditionally preferred to do business (Ashkenas, DeMonaco, and Francis, 1998).

How can firms consciously change their culture? During the last two decades a number of different approaches have been outlined for changing corporate culture. Several representative approaches include Kilmann's five steps for closing culture gaps, Trice and Beyer's use of organizational rites, Sethia and Von Glinow's use of reward systems, and Schein's set of strategies based on the life cycle stage of an organization. To give you a flavor for some of these archetypal approaches to cultural change, each of these methods is briefly discussed.

Five Steps for Closing Culture Gaps

Kilmann's (1989, 1985) approach is aimed at surfacing and changing cultural norms. Norms are a good place to begin a cultural change effort because they are universal, necessary, and relatively malleable. The first step in this process is to identify current norms operating within a group. This can be done informally or through the use of a standardized instrument called the Kilmann-Saxton (1983) Culture Gap Survey. Next, the target group needs to discuss where the organization is headed and what general types of behavior will be necessary for it to be successful in the future. Working with this information, a new set of more desirable norms is listed. The difference between the current norms and the desired norms provides the basis for a culture gap analysis. In the Kilmann-Saxton instrument the focus of the gap analysis is centered on four such norms that have been shown to be universally present in organizations. These norms include task support, or norms about sharing information, helping others, and being concerned with efficiency; task innovation, that is, norms for being creative and doing new things; social relationships, seen in norms for socializing with others at work and mixing work and friendship; and personal freedom, which looks at issues like expressing oneself and being able to use discretion. Whether these data are generated informally or through the use of the formal survey, the fifth step in the process is for the group to use the gap analysis as a basis for developing a detailed action plan about how it will change its behavior in the future and a method to track its progress along the way.

Using Organizational Rites to Change a Culture

Trice and Beyer (1985) have suggested that, when used creatively, organizational rites can also become useful ways to promote cultural change for two reasons. First, rites are a natural part of the organizational landscape, so they can be easily used as an occasion to express and promote important organizational values. Second, all rites simultaneously serve both practical and expressive purposes; thus, they can readily serve multiple purposes.

More precisely, Trice and Beyer identified six distinctive rites that they felt are worthy of consideration as potential cultural management tools. Two of these rites, which work naturally together, are the rites of "passage" and "enhancement." A rite of passage consists of the interview and orientation process that allows a select group of individuals to join the firm. Rites of enhancement occur as individuals are selected out of the organization for special recognition. Organizations like Mary Kay Cosmetics have elevated both of these rites to an art form that quickly binds new members to the organization's core values and cements this relationship with more long-standing members.

A third important rite, "degradation," is distinctively different from the first two in its purpose and intent. Sparingly used as a cultural management tool, this rite is nonetheless important because it can signal who does not fit in the culture and therefore must go. The most notable recent example of how this tool can be used was in the highly publicized firing of Coke's new CEO Doug Ivester. As detailed in a feature article in *Fortune* (Tarpley, 2000), Ivester was forced to resign by his two strongest board members, Warren Buffet and Herbert Allen, because of his lack of results and insensitivity to the cultural demands for collegiality with the firm's major bottlers. It seems that for all of his brilliance, Ivester just did not understand that the powers behind the scene did not want a one-man high-wire act running their business.

Two additional rites that often are used together are around "conflict resolution" and "integration." These rites center on the need to create a work environment that allows different factions within a firm to work together toward common goals. Classic examples here are the need for union(s) and management to express their differences and yet still find effective ways to work together and the need for ways to allow all members of an organization to celebrate their unity through all-company events.

The sixth rite identified by Trice and Beyer was called "renewal." Of all the rites, this is probably the least useful as a tool for cultural change because it is aimed primarily at celebrating the current order. It is often the focus of many so-called retreats. It is useful to firms because it provides a platform for individuals to express their positive feelings toward the organization and hopes for a brighter future, but it is rarely a driver for major culture change within an organization.

Aligning Culture and Reward Systems

Another potential way to change a culture is to look at the match between organizational values and the reward system within the firm to determine how well they are aligned. More specifically, in analyzing the ways that organizations have developed systems for matching their cultures and rewards (i.e., financial, job content, career development, status), Sethia and Von Glinow (1985) discovered four generic alignment patterns. These patterns, based on how much concern that firms have for people and performance, were described by the authors as follows. Some organizations do not show much concern for their people or their performance. These firms were called "apathetic" by the authors because they neither emphasize people development nor provide rewards for doing a good job. A second cluster of firms shows considerable concern for their people, but limited interest in performance. These firms were labeled as "caring" in the sense that there was ample job security for employees but little rewards for going the extra mile. They called another cluster of firms "exacting" because they had very high performance standards yet showed little concern for their people. In these environments, employees were well rewarded as long as they performed but discarded as soon as they faltered. The fourth group of firms were called "integrative." These organizations cared about the long-term growth and development of their people and recognized outstanding performance in many ways.

These patterns speak to the fact that culture and rewards are highly interdependent. When they are in alignment, different outcomes will result, albeit ones that are in harmony with the firm's hopes and expectations. On the other hand, when they are inconsistent, mixed messages will be sent throughout the workplace that will lead to confusion and frustration. By making adjustments in the reward system, therefore, it is possible to more clearly reflect the core values that an organization hopes to exhibit.

Basing Culture Change Strategies on Life Cycle Stages

Another perspective on culture change can be gained from looking at how the function of culture changes throughout the life cycle of an organization and thus how the culture needs to be managed over time. For example, Schein (1985) has noted that culture plays a different role in the life of a group as it matures.

At the time of its birth and early growth, one of the most critical functions of culture is to give a sense of identity to the group. Therefore, cultural interventions at this stage may often need to be aimed at clarifying the basic tenets that will form the foundation for the group's efforts. Later, at midlife, when the firm is expanding into new markets and products, cultural integration may decline, and a variety of subcultures begin to appear. To address this challenge, managers need to gain deeper insight into the content of their culture and the disintegration process that is under way to decide what elements of the older culture need to be maintained and what to let go, to be replaced with more appropriate values. Finally, when the firm moves into maturity, some parts of the culture may have become truly dysfunctional. Here, interventions must be aimed at surfacing and attacking often deeply held assumptions that are preventing the organization from growing.

In summary, changing a corporate culture is not an easy task. On the other hand, given an appreciation for the nature of culture, it is not an impossible task either. There are many methods available for making a cultural transition happen. The key to success is in matching the right approach to the issue(s) of concern. When a good fit has been made, the change effort may feel like a rocket blasting off. At first, all you hear and see is the noise, smoke, and fire. However, if the rocket has been well designed and has a well-developed guidance mechanism and a talented control team to monitor its progress, then the tension-filled launch will be followed by a graceful trajectory into a future marked by increasing speed and decreasing resistance.

CREATING A CONTINUOUS IMPROVEMENT WORK ENVIRONMENT

We now turn to the central question of this chapter, namely, why it is essential for a supportive culture to be created as a precondition for the development of a quality organization. To begin gaining a deeper appreciation for why this is so, it is useful to recognize that every day organizations face, and must deal effectively with, two general classes of problems (Heifetz, 1998, 1994). Some of these problems are essentially technical in nature. For example, introducing a new version of a standard software package is essentially a technical problem. Everyone will moan and groan about the need to learn some new formats and techniques, but only the mechanics that are behind how work gets done have been changed. The way that employees think about their job and how they behave have not really been challenged. So, conventional problem-solving methods like project management tools and techniques are usually sufficient to make these changes happen.

The other problems to be addressed are adaptive or cultural in nature. These problems are much more difficult to address because they demand that employees change not only the mechanics of how they do their work but also the way they think about their work and how they behave toward others (Garvin, 1995). For example, in some public sector agencies such as the Department of Motor Vehicles customers have been historically viewed and treated as a necessary inconvenience. Getting employees in these organizations to begin thinking that serving customers is why they are in business and treating customers with respect will always be a significant challenge (Fairfield-Sonn, 1993).

Given the nature of cultural norms and values, not surprisingly, they are often more challenging to manage and change than purely technical concerns (Ott, 1989). Quite frankly, it should be anticipated that any effort aimed at altering them will require substantial time, very clear communication, and visible reinforcement from management before any significant impact will be seen. Certainly, moving from a traditional, bureaucratic style of management, to a continuous quality improvement approach ranks as one of the greatest adaptive changes that any firm can take on. Indeed, this change may require a multistage process, described later, for creating a whole new image of what the organization is all about (Garvin, 1995; Morgan, 1986).

Diagnosis of Current Conditions

To build a quality organization, you need three high-level skills. One skill is the ability to conduct an accurate diagnosis of current conditions within the organization. Specifically, this diagnosis must look closely at two issues. One issue is the current cultural orientation within the firm. As shown in Figure 2.3 , this assessment needs to focus on determining the degree to which

the firm currently embraces traditional values (e.g., the importance of tightly controlling people and budgets within a hierarchical structure) versus continuous improvement values (e.g., the
importance of controlling processes within a flat, cross-functional
structure) (Denison, Hart, and Kahn, 1996; Deming, 1986). See
Chapter 3 for more information on these differences. The other
issue, which has received more attention to date but, as argued
here, is actually of lesser importance, is the current level of technical knowledge that members of the firm have about how to use
a growing variety of quality improvement tools and techniques.

Developing an Appropriate Change Strategy

The second skill is the ability to devise an appropriate
change strategy based on your diagnosis of current conditions.
Once you know where the organization falls on these two dimensions, then a variety of tailored change strategies can be
crafted. For example, since Firm A in Figure 2.3 already embraces a continuous improvement philosophy, but no one has
been extensively trained in the tools and techniques for making
process improvements, this firm's change strategy should focus
on offering a series of very application-oriented workshops in
preparation for completion of projects within the organization.
The firm is ready to begin its quest for quality in earnest.

In contrast, Firm B needs to begin by gaining a deeper understanding of the philosophy of continuous improvement. In
particular, the senior management team needs to spend considerable time on this issue to decide if it wants to become truly
committed to a new way of running the business (Garvin, 1995).
If it concludes from this review that the effort would be worthwhile, then review sessions on the philosophy as well as the tools
and techniques of continuous improvement would be beneficial
to get the effort under way.

In Firm C we see another scenario. Members of this organization have the knowledge to make process improvements, but it
is unlikely that much progress is being made or will ever be
made until several critical cultural questions are resolved. This is
the type of situation where, over time, employees often come to

view the quality effort cynically. That is, it is just another in a long series of management fads that will soon pass into organizational history. This is a serious situation for the firm and one where cultural issues should be squarely addressed before devoting any more resources to the effort.

Figure 2.3
Building a Quality Organization

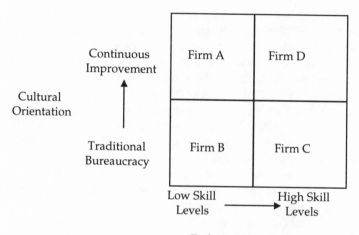

Technical Knowledge of
Quality Improvement Methods

Firm D is already well under way in its quest for quality. Accordingly, its efforts should reflect a balance between finding ways to drive the quality orientation deeper into the fabric of the organization (e.g., enhancing critical rites within the firm such that their value orientation is more visible) and devoting resources to learning more advanced quality improvement methods (e.g., running six-sigma projects).

Clearly, each of the archetypal firms in Figure 2.3 is starting in a different place, and that is fine. As discussed in Chapter 1, all firms share the common fate that over time their quality standards will continue to climb. As a consequence, regardless of the level of quality that a firm can deliver today, it must constantly evaluate what level of quality must be provided in the future to best its competition and then, working with this understanding, to establish what quality standards it intends to pursue. Depending on the nature and size of the gap between their current and desired performance, different change strategies should be employed, as appropriate to the demands of the situation.

Enhancing the Capacity to Learn from the Experience

The third key skill is to create a capacity among, and willingness by, employees to learn from their process improvement experiences such that the drive toward higher quality becomes just the way we do business here. Why is this so important? It will be recalled that one of the greatest work process improvement innovations of all time was the assembly line. This innovation made Ford a very rich company at the turn of the last century. Yet, in the 1920s General Motors pulled ahead of Ford in revenues and profitability based on a complex set of business process innovations that led to the creation of what came to be known as the modern-day hierarchical bureaucracy. This model, in turn, held sway until the 1980s, when the Japanese demonstrated that there were even better ways to run and organize a company. Today, more advances in process management continue to emerge in the form of the drive for six-sigma levels of quality and the use of increasingly sophisticated software packages to run ever more competitive organizations, to name just a few. What lesson can we draw from this experience? Simply that good works today will not guarantee success tomorrow. Only those organizations whose culture rewards a passion for learning and building systems to convert information into working knowledge will thrive for the long term (Baldrige National Quality Program, 2000).

In summary, if the pursuit of continuous improvement is an excellent habit shared by all quality organizations, then it can be fairly said that they are united, in part, by a similar cultural mind-set. To use Deal and Kennedy's typology, they are a tribe. Although companies within this tribe operate in very different industries and produce a widely diverse set of products and services, they nonetheless display profound similarities in the way that they approach everyday problems. They share many elements of a common philosophy. They have a common language that allows them to communicate easily with each other. They understand each other's struggles and desires. They will attack their unique problems with similar tools, techniques, and methodologies. Given these commonalities, they have some enormous advantages over nontribe members. For example, they can learn more quickly from each other's experiences, and, where appropriate, they can form beneficial partnerships more readily. In this sense, they are more agile learners, and this learning advantage compounds to their benefit over time in the form of enhanced organizational, team, and individual performance.

REFERENCES

Ashkenas, R. N., DeMonaco, L. J. & Francis, S. C. 1998. Making the deal real: How GE Capital integrates acquisitions. *Harvard Business Review*, 76 (1): 165–178.

Baldrige National Quality Program, 2000. *Criteria for performance excellence.* Washington, D.C.: NIST.

Bauman, R. P., Jackson, P. & Lawrence, J. T. 1997. *From promise to performance: A journey of transformation at SmithKline Beecham.* Boston: Harvard Business School Press.

Buono, A. F., & Bowditch, J. L. 1989. *The human side of mergers and acquisitions.* San Francisco: Jossey-Bass.

Collins, J. C., and Porras, J. I. 1994. *Built to last: Successful habits of visionary companies.* New York: Harper Business.

Davis, S. M. 1984. *Managing corporate culture.* Cambridge, MA: Ballinger.

Deal, T. E., & Kennedy, A. A. 1982. *Corporate cultures: The rites and rituals of corporate life.* Reading, MA: Addison-Wesley.

de Geus, A. 1997. The Living Company. *Harvard Business Review*, 75 (2): 51–59.

Deming. W. E. 1986. *Out of the crisis.* Cambridge: MIT Center for Advanced Engineering Study.

Denison, D. R., Hart, S. L. & Kahn, J. A. 1996. From chimneys to cross-functional teams: Developing and validating a diagnostic model. *Academy of Management Journal*, 39 (4): 1005–1023.

Fairfield-Sonn, J. W. 1993. Moving beyond vision: Fostering cultural change in a bureaucracy. *Journal of Organizational Change Management*, 6 (5): 43–55.

Fairfield-Sonn, J. W. 1984. What is your organization's I.Q.? *Municipal Management*, 6 (4): 127–131.

Garvin, D. A. 1995. Leveraging processes for strategic advantage: A roundtable with Xerox's Allaire, USAA's Herres, SmithKline Beecham's Leschly, and Pepsi's Weatherup. *Harvard Business Review*, 73 (5): 77–90.

Hackman, J. R. (Ed.). 1990. *Groups that work (and those that don't)*. San Francisco: Jossey-Bass.

Heifetz, R. A. 1998. Walking the fine line of leadership. *The Journal for Quality and Participation*, 21 (1): 8–14.

Heifetz, R. A. 1994. *Leadership without easy answers*. Cambridge: Harvard University Press.

Inc. 1999. The culture wars. May 18: 107.

Katzenbach, J. R., & Smith, D. K. 1993. *The wisdom of teams: Creating the high-performance organization*. Boston: Harvard Business School Press.

Kilmann, R. H. 1989. *Managing beyond the quick fix: A completely integrated program for creating and maintaining organizational success*. San Francisco: Jossey-Bass.

Kilmann, R. H. 1985. Five steps for closing culture-gaps. In Kilmann, R. H., Saxton, M. J., Serpa, R. & Associates (Eds.), *Gaining control of the corporate culture*. 351–369. San Francisco: Jossey-Bass.

Kilmann, R. H., & Saxton, M. J. 1983. *The Kilmann-Saxton Culture Gap Survey*. Pittsburgh, PA: Organizational Design Consultants.

Kotter, J. P., & Heskett, J. L. 1992. *Corporate culture and performance*. New York: Free Press.

Mohrman, S. A., Cohen, S. G. & Mohrman, A. M., Jr. 1995. *Designing team-based organizations: New forms for knowledge work*. San Francisco: Jossey-Bass.

Morgan, G. 1986. *Images of organization*. Beverly Hills, CA: Sage.

Morgan, S., & Dennehy, R. F. 1997. The power of organizational storytelling: A management development perspective. *Journal of Management Development*, 16 (7): 494–501.

Neuhauser, P. C. 1993. *Corporate legends and lore*. New York: McGraw-Hill.

Ott, J. S. 1989. *The organizational culture perspective*. Chicago: Irwin.

Peters, T. J., & Waterman, R. H, Jr. 1982. *In search of excellence: Lessons from America's best-run companies*. New York: Harper & Row.

Raspa, R. 1990. The CEO as corporate myth-maker: Negotiating the boundaries of work and play at Domino's Pizza. In Gagliardi, P. (Ed.), *Symbols and artifacts: Views of the corporate landscape.* 273–279. Berlin: de Gruyter.

Schein, E. H. 1985. *Organizational culture and leadership.* San Francisco: Jossey-Bass.

Sethia, N. K., & Von Glinow, M. A. 1985. Arriving at four cultures by managing the reward systems. In Kilmann, R. H., Saxton, M. J., Serpa, R. & Associates (Eds.), *Gaining control of the corporate culture.* 400–420. San Francisco: Jossey-Bass.

Tarpley, N. A. 2000. What really happened at Coke. *Fortune,* January 10: 114–116.

Trice, H. M., & Beyer, J. M. 1985. Using six organizational rites to change culture. In Kilmann, R. H., Saxton, M. J., Serpa, R. & Associates (Eds.), *Gaining control of the corporate culture.* 370–399. San Francisco: Jossey-Bass.

Weber, Y. 1996. Corporate cultural fit and performance in mergers and acquisitions. *Human Relations,* 49 (9): 1181–1202.

Building a Foundation
for Quality

A journey of a thousand miles begins with a single
step.

—Chinese Proverb

Building a high-quality organization is like constructing a house.
If you want the structure to last, start with a solid foundation. To
create the foundation for a quality organization, three key tasks
need attention. Two of these activities have already been discussed in some detail. Specifically, you need to articulate a vision
that embraces quality as central to the long-term success of the
organization and to promote a cultural mind-set that will clearly
support efforts aimed at quality improvement. The third key
element, which is the primary focus of this chapter, is to create
an integrated set of strategic systems that are capable of convert-
ing the promise of ever improving quality into daily practice and
performance.

WHAT DO WE WANT TO BECOME?

Vision speaks to *what* the organization is trying to become in the long-term future (Collins and Porras, 1996, 1994). A vision is important in the sense that it is the "North Star" from which the whole organization determines its current position and calculates its future direction.

Many organizations have so-called vision statements, but they are little more than a handful of overused words on a piece of paper. In contrast, high-quality organizations often have simple, distinctive vision statements. For example, Ford's vision, "Quality is Job #1," or Bechtel's vision, "We will build anything, anywhere, at any time," is unique and inspiring. Other firms, such as the very successful nonprofit Nature Conservancy, are guided by a more elaborate vision statement: "To preserve plants, animals and natural communities that represent the diversity of life on Earth by protecting the lands and the waters they need to survive." What all these statements have in common, however, is that they speak to the desire to attain greatness in a chosen field of endeavor, and thus they are motivating and energizing forces within each of these organizations.

To appreciate the power of vision to help bring about a quality transformation, consider the following illustrative story. In the early 1980s, Celanese Corporation began a quality revolution using many of the techniques that were being developed in Japan. At a high-level meeting the director for quality was making a presentation on 20 areas where progress on quality improvement was being measured. At one point in the presentation, John Macomber, the CEO, leaned back in his chair and asked this famous question: "We're at a stage where we'd rate about a 3 on a scale of 10. But I'm not as interested in where we are as in where we're going. What I'd like to know is what 10 out of 10 would look like." Everyone at the meeting agreed that it was a great question, and the director of quality promised to develop an answer. This led to the creation of the "Ten Out of Ten" document, which subsequently served as a vision for where the firm would be moving in the future. Indeed, this statement was so powerful that it continued to provide guidance to the firm even after its merger with Hoechst.

HOW MUCH DO WE BELIEVE IN OUR VALUES?

Culture speaks to *how* a firm will produce its products or deliver its services. Of the three elements that form a platform for significant quality improvement, it is the most often overlooked and its power least understood. Ironically, it is also the area where the greatest potential for major improvement in quality often lies. The reason for this oversight is simple. Most quality decisions are not made in an executive suite. Rather, the vast majority of quality decisions are made in everyday settings where employees make decisions about how much quality to put into a firm's products and services.

There is a wonderful story from France that makes this point very well. One day a French priest came upon a work site at a remote monastery. There he found three workers laying bricks. When he asked the first worker what he was doing, the worker said, "I am laying one brick next to the other." Approaching the second worker, the priest again inquired what he was doing. To the question this worker replied, "I'm building a wall." Moving on to the third worker, the priest again inquired what he was doing. This time the reply was, "I am building a cathedral to the glory of God." From the workers' answers it is clear that they all understood what they were doing, but it is likewise easy to see that *how* they were approaching the task was fundamentally different.

This French monastery story can serve as a useful metaphor to understand how leaders from different organizations have approached the quest for quality improvement and why their results have been so varied. For some leaders, quality is just laying another brick in a courtyard. For other leaders, quality will provide them with a new wall of strength. Yet, for others, quality is the means to build something bigger and better than what previously existed. While all three approaches will lead to improvements in quality, the magnitude of the quality enhancement will obviously vary widely.

HOW WELL CAN WE EXECUTE?

In a recent *Fortune* article Charan and Colvin (1999) reported on their analysis of why CEOs fail. The single most important reason was the failure to execute. In other words, it is important to know what you want to do (i.e., the vision), and how you want to do it (i.e., the culture), but without the systems capability to execute (i.e., the strategic management systems) an organization will fail to reach its full potential because of its inability to make optimal use of all the available resources. In other words, while quality improvement is an invaluable organizing concept, it must be converted into an integrated set of practices that all of the employees within a firm deeply embrace, or little will come from it (Cole, Bacdayan, and White, 1993).

Fortunately, all three of these activities are within the reach of every organization whose management team has a passion for making it happen. It is important to note at the outset though, that these elements are also intimately interrelated. That is, in practice, each of the elements will combine with the other two to define the basic character of the larger organizational system (Deming, 1986), the final result being a tapestry of interlinked parts that adds up to something greater than the sum of the parts (Figure 3.1).

You should also know that when done right, the long-term rewards for building a quality organization can be significant. For instance, a study by the National Institute of Standards and Technology (NIST) found that publicly traded Malcolm Baldrige Quality Award-winning companies, the so-called "Baldrige Index," outperformed the Standard & Poor's (S & P) 500 by a margin of 2.6 to 1 during the years 1988 to 1997. That is, if you invested $1,000 in each of the Baldrige Award-winning companies when it was announced and $1,000 in the S & P 500, your respective rates of return on these investments would have been 460% versus 175% (NIST, 1999).

While the returns on investments in quality can be substantial, it also needs to be recognized that quality improvements will not come without the commitment of time, money, and deep personal involvement. Moreover, the road will not always be easy.

Figure 3.1
Linking Vision, Culture, and Strategic Management Systems

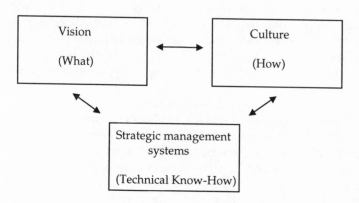

To enhance quality, therefore, it is necessary for senior management, in particular, to develop a broad view of how all the parts of its organization are interconnected as well as a passion to constantly improve several key quality management practices. At a minimum, this will require that all members of the top management team will need to encourage positive attitudes toward quality and to actively support efforts to teach employees how to use standard quality improvement tools and techniques (Procopio and Fairfield-Sonn, 1996). Yet, more importantly, the senior team must become dedicated stewards of the overall effort by creating an integrated vision, culture, and set of strategic management systems to ensure that work on behalf of process improvement is consistently recognized and rewarded (Fairfield-Sonn, 1999). For example, L.L. Bean has recognized the importance of outstanding customer service for a long time and has worked hard to instill this value in its employees, but it has also invested heavily in a vast, well-integrated information system to make it happen.

Ritz-Carlton Hotels

Another good example of how the three foundation elements have been successfully integrated can be found in the Ritz-Carlton Hotel Company. This firm, based in Atlanta, manages 36 luxury hotels worldwide. With approximately 17,000 employees, its revenues in 1998 were more than $1 billion. The Ritz-Carlton is notable in that it is the only service company to receive the Baldrige Award twice.

The Ritz-Carlton, which was founded in 1984 on the principle of providing groundbreaking levels of customer service, has the easy-to-understand vision "We are ladies and gentlemen serving ladies and gentlemen." In addition, its core values have been clearly captured in what it calls "The Gold Standards," which consists of its "Credo," "The Three Steps of Service," "The Motto," and "The Twenty Basics." These core values are extensively used in the selection, orientation, and ongoing training of all employees to reinforce their basic beliefs and to energize the efforts of all employees to provide outstanding levels of customer service.

The tremendous success enjoyed by this firm, however, would not be possible without a dense network of interconnected strategic systems that it has developed over the years to support the efforts of every employee to delight customers. For example, it has created an innovative customer database to record guests' preferences and customize services to meet these preferences. With this database, consisting of nearly 1 million customer files available on-line worldwide to support the goal of anticipating guest needs, it has a powerful tool to increase customer loyalty and retention. Employees have also been empowered to spend up to $2,000 to immediately correct or handle any customer complaint. In addition, all of its key processes (e.g., reservations) are directly linked to key performance measures (e.g., customer survey ratings), which, in turn, are derived from its "vital few" objectives (e.g., improving guest satisfaction). Moreover, all of these processes are constantly managed and being improved by process owners and quality improvement teams.

LEARNING FROM OTHERS—MALCOLM BALDRIGE QUALITY AWARDS

If you have decided that it would be worthwhile to adopt a more systematic approach to improving quality within your organization, there is some good news waiting for you. First, you do not have to create a model for how to improve your quality from scratch. Second, there is much advice available either on how to get started or on how to take your effort to a higher level. Third, much of this advice can be obtained at relatively little or no cost to your firm.

Guidance

The reason for this good news is that in 1987 the U.S. government created a unique public-private partnership aimed at improving the competitiveness of American firms (Public Law 100-107). This effort is officially known as the Malcolm Baldrige National Quality Award, MBNQA, program. Administered by the National Institute of Standards and Technology (NIST), an agency within the Department of Commerce, this program was designed to fulfill three purposes. One purpose is to help improve organizational performance practices and capabilities. The second goal is to facilitate communication and sharing of best practices information among all types of U.S. organizations. The third intent is to provide working tools for understanding and managing performance as well as methods for guiding planning and training.

To achieve its purposes, the MBNQA program has developed and continually refines a system for helping firms to improve their business results in five key areas. These areas are improvement in customer focus, financial and market results, developing human resources, building more effective partnerships, and overall organizational effectiveness.

Moreover, this system is based on a clearly stated set of core values and concepts. These ideas include the importance of fostering more visionary leadership, becoming more customer-driven, consciously pursuing organizational and personal learning, valuing employees and partners, encouraging agility, managing for innovation, management by fact, public responsibility and good citizenship, a focus on results and creating value, and adopting a systems perspective (Baldrige National Quality Program, 2000).

Assessment

To make progress on the quality journey, it is useful to have milestones along the way to know where you are, how far you have come, and how far you need to go. Fortunately, because of extensive efforts on the part of the MBNQA program it is not necessary to guess how well you are doing compared to other organizations. Over the last decade a comprehensive assessment methodology, based on a 1,000-point scoring system, has been constantly evolving at the national level and replicated in large part by around 40 state and numerous local-level organizations to provide firms with an in-depth read on how well they are doing with their quality efforts.

This assessment, which reflects all of the core values and concepts of the MBNQA program, is structured around the seven evaluation categories that constitute the Baldrige performance excellence framework (Figure 3.2).

The framework itself has three basic elements: strategy and action plans, the system, and information and analysis. More precisely, strategy and action plans (top of the figure) yield the set of customer- and market-focused performance requirements, derived from short- and long-term strategic planning, that must be met or exceeded for an organization's strategy to succeed. The system comprises the six Baldrige categories in the center of the figure that define the organization, its operations, and its results. Leadership (category 1), strategic planning (category 2), and customer and market focus (category 3) represent the leadership triad. These categories are placed together to emphasize the importance of a leadership focus on strategy and customers. Human resource focus (category 5), process management (category 6), and business results (category 7) represent the results triad. An organization's employees and its key processes accomplish the work of the organization that yields the observed results. Finally, information and analysis (category 4) serve as a foundation for the performance management system by providing facts to be used in improving performance.

Figure 3.2
Malcolm Baldrige Performance Excellence Framework

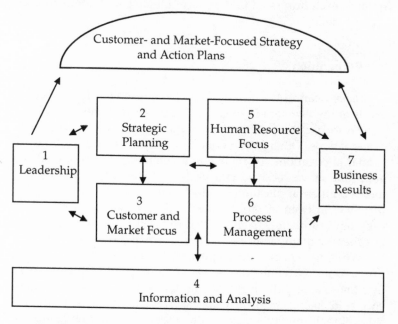

Feedback

How well a firm is doing in each category is evaluated under the MBNQA program guidelines based on the written responses from a firm as they address a standard set of questions. In other words, the MBNQA program assessment does not tell firms how they should approach their quality improvement effort. Rather, it indicates how well a firm's answers reflect an integrated, goals-oriented approach to reaching whatever targets the firm is attempting to meet and what further opportunities for improvement might exist based on what it has been told.

The assessment then, which is developed by trained examiners, senior examiners, and judges, as appropriate, leads to a detailed report on how well the company appears to be doing in each of the seven areas based on the firm's own views. The primary value to be derived from this type of feedback is its usefulness in helping the firm to ask better questions of itself in the future. Meanwhile, there are no prescriptions by the reviewers because each firm must find its own unique path to performance enhancement.

Recognition

Since its inception, many firms have benefited from various levels of involvement in the MBNQA program. Some firms have chosen to use the program's materials merely for internal self-examinations. Others have gone to the next step and submitted formal applications for review and comment. The best of these applicants have received site visits to confirm the firm's statements on their application and to clarify issues that are not completely clear from the application materials. Only 37 firms, however, have ultimately been selected to receive this coveted award in either the manufacturing, service, or small business categories.

Winning carries with it great pride and recognition for the firm and just two obligations. One requirement of all winners is that they participate in the annual Quest for Excellence conference held each year in early spring. There the winners share the story of their quality journey with others. The other obligation is to share nonproprietary information from their application with other firms, whether or not they attended the conference, that are interested in learning more about how to improve their own quality efforts.

Why the MBNQA Works

There are many reasons that this model works. Paul De-Baylo, a former senior Baldrige examiner, has recently identified at least 10 of these (DeBaylo, 1999). These reasons for success are as follows.

1. *Assessment and improvements drive business results.* After over 12 years in operation it is now clear that the process produces results. As evidenced by the Baldrige Index, quality companies see the results of their efforts in a broad array of bottom-line results.

2. *Criteria that encourage concepts and values.* Using the Baldrige approach encourages firms to understand and use the core concepts and values to produce an integrated approach to moving the entire enterprise forward to higher levels of quality.

3. *Customized improvement models.* Companies can tailor the general model to their own unique needs, but understanding how the whole model works helps everyone in the organization to better understand how his or her individual contributions support the overall effort.

4. *Pervasive use of self-assessment.* In the past it was extremely difficult to develop a true organization-wide assessment. The Baldrige criteria allow firms to see how many parts of their operation are connected and how these relationships help to explain why performance is or is not improving.

5. *Recognition drives participation.* Many firms have used internal Baldrige-like assessments to recognize progress being made within the firm. When properly structured, these systems can produce lots of winners, who are, in turn, more interested in further participation.

6. *Assessment is linked to business strategies.* Assessment by itself is of little value. When assessment is linked to improvements in business results, the motivation to engage in the effort mounts.

7. *Senior management involvement.* One of the most effective ways to get senior management to buy in to the effort is to create networks among executives who are interested in improving quality with those who have already done so.

8. *Accelerated learning.* One of the most effective ways to promote learning is by doing. Promoting active involvement

in all phases of the assessment process can lead to significant new learnings.

9. *Criteria evolve and improve*. The Baldrige criteria are not static. Over time, the criteria evolve and become more effective as participants and examiners grow in their knowledge of how to enhance progress on the quality journey.

10. *One size doesn't fit all*. Over time firms have learned to become more creative about how to use the criteria to meet their unique needs. Some firms like to use the criteria as audits. Other firms prefer to use the criteria as the basis for an internal consulting opportunity. How the criteria are used are less important than that they get employees to start thinking how the key concepts and values can allow them to improve their processes and performance.

MBNQA Program as a Cultural Phenomenon

While the MBNQA program has been praised and criticized over the years, from a cultural perspective it is hard to overestimate its importance as an institutionalizing force for change. Any organization that wants to be recognized as a quality leader must at a minimum be well versed on the views promulgated by this program. For those who wish to be officially recognized as a quality organization there is no option but to incorporate major concepts about continuous improvement, derived from the program's core values, into their thinking and operations. Quite simply, the MBNQA program articulates and represents the dominant philosophy and practices for bringing about significant change in thinking about how to improve quality. While it is reasonable to take exception with some aspects of the ideology, outright rejection of major principles would raise serious concerns about the commitment of an organization to the pursuit of quality improvement. For example, what company that says that it is interested in improving its quality would want to publicly challenge the idea that a firm should be customer-focused?

In addition to promulgating a distinctive set of values and recognizing those who embrace them, the MBNQA program at the national, state, and local levels also plays a major role in identifying, selecting, and socializing individuals and firms into a distinctive set of rites, rituals, and traditions that bind the quality improvement community together (Crownover, Bush, and Darrouzet, 1999). Foremost among these rites and rituals is the annual Quest for Excellence conference. As the organizers so clearly state, "This three-day conference is designed to maximize learning and networking opportunities." Yet, gala events like the annual conference owe much of their success to the support and guidance provided earlier in the quality journey by enthusiasts like Sheila Carmine, president, Connecticut Quality Improvement Award Partnership. She created the first state-level quality recognition program in 1987 as a means to encourage the initial participation of individuals and firms in this effort. Now there are 55 state, regional, and local quality award programs. From these deep roots, the tree grows stronger each year.

In summary, to build a quality organization, you need to start with a solid foundation. That foundation consists of three deeply intertwined elements, namely, a quality vision, a quality culture, and strategic management systems. All three are vital to the success of the endeavor. A weakness in any one of these elements will sap strength from the other two. When all three are strong, however, a special synergy develops that can lead to outstanding performance and pride in a job well done.

REFERENCES

Baldrige National Quality Program, 2000. *Criteria for Performance Excellence*. Washington, D. C.: NIST.

Charan, R., & Colvin, G. 1999. Why CEOs fail. *Fortune*. 139 (12): 68–72, 74, 76, 78.

Cole, R. E., Bacdayan, P. & White, B. J. 1993. Quality, participation, and competitiveness. *California Management Review*, 35 (3): 68–81.

Collins, J. C., & Porras, J. I. 1996. Building your company's vision. *Harvard Business Review*, 74 (5): 65–77.

Collins, J. C., & Porras, J. I. 1994. *Built to last: Successful practices of visionary companies*. New York: Harper Business.

Crownover, D., Bush, L. & Darrouzet, J. 1999. *Take it to the next level: A story of the quest for quality and the Malcolm Baldrige Award*. Dallas, TX: NextLevel Press.

DeBaylo, P. 1999. Ten reasons why the Baldrige model works. *The Journal for Quality & Participation*, 1: 1–5.

Deming, W. E. 1986. *Out of the crisis*. Cambridge: MIT Center for Advanced Engineering Study.

Fairfield-Sonn, J.W. 1999. Influence of context on process improvement teams: Leadership from a distance. *Journal of Business and Economic Studies*, 5 (2): 61–80.

Heifetz, R. A. 1998. Walking the fine line of leadership. *The Journal for Quality and Participation*, 21 (1): 8–14.

Heifetz, R. A. 1994. *Leadership without easy answers*. Cambridge: Harvard University Press.

NIST. 1999. Baldrige Index' 67 outperforms S&P 500 for fifth year. February 4: 1–2.

Procopio, A. J., & Fairfield-Sonn, J. W. 1996. Changing attitudes towards quality: An exploratory study. *Group & Organization Management*, 21 (2): 133–145.

Public Law 100-107. The Malcolm Baldrige national quality improvement act of 1987.

Part II

Making Quality Happen

Chapter 4

Making Quality a Strategic Priority

> At general management's core is strategy: defining a company's position, making trade-offs, and forging fit among activities.
>
> —Michael Porter, 1996

If you hope to build a quality organization, strategic planning is an essential tool to make it happen. How you decide to use this tool, however, will go a long way toward determining how much value you will get from it. For example, if you decide to make strategic planning into an annual "rite of renewal" resulting in the publication of a summary document that is quickly and quietly put away until the next year or an "iron cage" that must be meticulously followed even when unexpected events occur, the payback for everyone's time and effort will be minimal. On the other hand, if you see strategic planning as a vital way to raise and debate competing visions of the firm and how the resulting vision could best be implemented throughout the organization, then the rewards can be enormous.

STRATEGIC PLANNING AS A LEARNING PROCESS

If you want to discover how deeply embedded strategic planning is in the culture of a firm, conduct a simple employee survey with just three questions. First, on a five-point scale from (5) excellent to (1) none, ask employees to describe their knowledge of the current strategic plan. Second, ask employees how much linkage they see between their individual work efforts and the firm's overall strategy. Third, ask to what degree an individual employee's compensation is based on the attainment of the firm's overall strategic goals and objectives.

The results, in most cases, will be sobering. The truth is that most employees, including even some of those who were involved in the formal strategic planning meetings, are usually only somewhat clear on the key points of the current strategy and how it will be implemented. When pushed, some may be able to offer a document that summarizes the plan, but that is hardly the same as understanding the strategy.

In quality firms, the strategy is summarized in a document. Yet, the strategy is much more than a written document. The strategy is a "living" guide for setting priorities around daily activities as well as how these priorities will be carried out.

In other words, there are many views on the purpose of strategic planning and how it should be conducted (Mintzberg, 1994). Within quality organizations, the dominant view is that this activity is foremost as an opportunity for leaders and managers *to learn* (de Geus, 1988) more about the organization and its place in its market(s) (Finkelstein and Hambrick, 1996). That is, it is important for key members of the organization to periodically examine what they hope the organization will become; to detail priorities for the future; and to clarify how the organization must change to meet future challenges. In completing this important work, a unique *strategic perspective* (Porter, 1996) emerges that reflects the organization's *vision* (Collins and Porras, 1996, 1994) of its values, principles, strengths, and opportunities within the context of marketplace realities.

An effective strategic planning effort also affords an opportunity for management to assess how well the organization is structured to pursue its goals. This critical activity is often called *organizational alignment* (Mohrman, Cohen, and Mohr- man, 1995; Galbraith, Lawler, and Associates, 1993). In practice, some planning reviews reveal that no adjustments are needed in the organization's structure or deployment of key members of the organization. Yet, other reviews make it obvious that restructuring and the assignment of new responsibilities will be a necessary precondition for the organization to successfully meet its challenges (Hamel and Prahalad, 1994; Prahalad and Hamel, 1990).

Another major value that can be derived from a strategic planning effort is to foster teamwork and to *enhance the motivation* (Cole, Bacdayan, and White, 1993) among members of the senior team to implement the plan. Indeed, this activity presents one of the best means for getting the entire senior management group to work cooperatively in the pursuit of common objectives (Hambrick and Mason, 1984). This end is achieved by allowing department leaders to develop a consensus about what needs to be done and how it needs to be accomplished. This understanding is particularly important when interdepartmental collaboration is necessary to reach organizational goals.

Finally, the strategic planning process can also provide an excellent opportunity for the organization to review its current systems for *recognizing and rewarding* behaviors (Sethia and Von Glinow, 1985). Every quality organization is concerned about motivating managers and employees to actively pursue its goals and objectives rather than personal agendas (Deming, 1986). Therefore, as a result of the planning process, it is possible and advisable to clarify exactly what kinds of behaviors are desired and then create appropriate reward mechanisms to ensure that they are reinforced.

Given the preceding perspective, the value to be derived from strategic planning comes both from making informed *choices* (Porter, 1996) and from asking critical *questions* (Argyris, 1994). In this way, strategic planning helps the organization to better position itself for today and the future. In answering these questions, members of the organization take ownership over what they want the organization to become and how these ends will be pursued.

QUALITY IMPROVEMENT AS A STRATEGIC OBJECTIVE

In Chapter 1, we discussed why you need to make choices about the level of quality (i.e., meeting expectations, exceeding expectations, delighting customers) that you will strive to offer customers. In Chapter 2, we discussed the importance of making conscious choices about the kind of culture (i.e., traditional hierarchical, bureaucracy versus continuous process improvement) that you want to foster in your firm. Here, we turn to a discussion about the role that quality improvement will play in the context of establishing a strategic *perspective* within the firm, and once again we find that choices must be made.

Choosing an Approach

More precisely, firms interested in improving the quality of their products and services have basically three different paths that they can follow in integrating quality into their strategic plans. One "consistent" approach is to identify one or more specific quality initiatives that should be undertaken during the course of the year. A more ambitious, "reinforcing" approach is to identify quality improvement as one of the principal goals of the organization. The third and most robust "optimizing" approach is to view quality improvement as a core value for the organization and thus something to be reflected in the "fit" among all the activities of the firm (Porter, 1996).

Return on the Investment

As Michael Porter (1996), one of the foremost writers on strategy today, has recently discussed, all of these approaches are worthwhile because they will undoubtedly improve a firm's organizational effectiveness. However, the return for your investment from these approaches will vary and thus may lead to some false conclusions about the real value that can be derived from devoting resources to improving the position of the organization in its marketplace through quality enhancement.

Specifically, when firms follow the first path, they may be disappointed to find that their efforts do not lead to a competitive advantage, but rather just the ability to stay current with the competition. The second approach will yield a greater return on investment for the firm because it will generate some synergies across a range of activities. In contrast, dramatic returns on investment will be seen only when quality improvement becomes a driving force behind the determination of what activities the company will perform, how they will perform them, and how all the firm's activities fit together (Porter, 1996).

Southwest Airlines as an Example

One of the best examples of the third approach is Southwest Airlines, which has been the only consistently profitable airline for the last 29 years and at or near the top of the *Fortune* "100 Best Companies to Work For" list during the last three years (Levering and Moskowitz, 2000). While widely recognized for its whacky and playful corporate culture, Herb Kelleher and his crew have a lot more going for them than just a fun day at work (de Geus, 1997; Nanus, 1992).

Perhaps the greatest advantage for this firm is that it recognized early on that the traditional hub-and-spoke model for organizing an airline, which is well suited for moving passengers around anywhere in the country, is not the only way that passengers like to travel (Drucker, 1994). There are some price- and convenience-sensitive passengers (e.g., business travelers, families, and students) who would prefer a short-haul, low-cost, point-to-point service between midsize cities and secondary airports if it meant that they could reach their destination at lower cost and with more convenience.

Obviously, not everyone prefers to travel in the Southwest style. However, once the leaders of the firm determined that there was a sufficiently large market for their type of services, they began building a new airline model based on doing different things and doing them differently. For example, in contrast to the "full-service" airlines that offer lots of comfort and amenities, Southwest tailors all its activities to deliver low-cost, convenient service on its routes. This means that on Southwest there are no meals, no assigned seats, and no special services. Moreover, passengers are encouraged to buy their tickets at the gate and thereby reduce the need for travel agent commissions.

Southwest realizes many cost advantages from not offering the services just mentioned. It also benefits from the fact that its simple model allows the company to turn airplanes in less than 15 minutes. This means that the airplanes are able to fly more hours than their competitors. In addition, since they use only a standardized fleet of 737 aircraft, their maintenance and inventory costs are reduced, while their learning curve for how best to work on this type of plane is increased.

While reducing costs in some areas, at the same time, Southwest invests heavily in others. Most notably, the company has been consistently generous with its employees, who are vital to making the operation run so efficiently. In particular, gate and ground crews have been paid much higher than industry standards for their work, and their profit-sharing plan and liberal use of stock options have already created dozens of Southwest millionaires (Levering and Moskowitz, 2000).

What do these specific examples and general discussion say about how quality improvement can improve firm performance? Quite simply, strategy is not primarily about finding new opportunities, but rather essentially about making choices around how to use limited resources to optimize results. To improve the quality of an organization's products and services, there must be a strategy and a plan on how this will be accomplished. Absent a strategy, it is highly unlikely that much progress will be made on this critical agenda. More importantly, to become recognized as a quality organization, it is not sufficient to just pursue isolated improvement opportunities or even to make quality improvement a separate corporate goal. Rather, quality improvement must be a central principle driving all the activities of the firm. In this way, quality improvement becomes a central organizing principle for the firm and ultimately the way of doing business.

CORE ELEMENTS IN THE STRATEGIC PLANNING PROCESS

Strategic planning is a process. Like every process it consists of a number of specific tasks that need to be accomplished to yield a final, useful, endproduct. The basic steps in this process were identified several decades ago (Bower, Bartlett, Uyterhoeven, and Walton, 1995; Hax and Majluf, 1991). Specifically, a strategic planning effort should begin with the creation or refinement of a common, long-term vision for the organization. Once this vision has been established, the organization needs to look carefully at its external markets in order to identify opportunities and threats (Porter, 1985, 1980) as well as to candidly assess the current internal strengths and weaknesses of the firm (Hamel and Prahalad, 1994; Prahalad and Hamel, 1990). Then, by simultaneously considering the dynamic interplay of the external and internal realities, a specific mission for the upcoming year can be created, which, in turn, can be translated into specific goals and measures of success.

Create a Long-Term Vision

The first and most important step in the strategic planning process is for the top management team to identify what the organization hopes to become in the long-term future. To answer this critical question, individuals involved in the planning process must clearly articulate what the firm hopes to become and its core values (Collins and Porras, 1996, 1994). These two component parts of the vision will, in turn, become the basis for theory of the business (Drucker, 1994).

To develop this vision, several simple, but very important, questions need to be addressed. For example, why are we in business? What are our basic values and principles? What kind of relationship do we want to foster with our customers, employees, suppliers, the community, and others with whom we do business? By exploring these vital questions, hopefully, a unique and compelling vision will emerge that will be meaningful, particularly for those inside the organization (Collins and Porras, 1996).

Assess the Organization's External Markets

With a clear vision of the future in mind, the planning group next needs to identify important opportunities and threats in the external marketplace (Porter, 1996, 1985, 1980). There are several parts to this analysis that collectively can yield some important insights. On the most macrolevel, this analysis can begin with the identification of economic, social, technological, and industry trends that could lead to opportunities or threats for the firm over the long term. Then, drilling down to the organizational level of analysis, a discussion needs to be generated about what market segments are currently being served and what special needs the products and/or services of the firm are filling in these markets (Pine and Gilmore, 1998). A closely related analysis needs to focus on what potential new markets exist and how the firm's products and/or services might also be valuable there. These reviews can then be followed by a competitive analysis to see how the firm's products and/or services rate compared to those of key competitors. This review will often reveal that the firm can offer more value to some customers than others (Treacy and Wiersema, 1993). Finally, a collaborator analysis can be useful to clarify what organizations might be potentially useful partners in the future (Kanter, 1994, 1989).

Evaluate Internal Capacity

Once the firm is clear on what external opportunities and threats are present in the marketplace, the next step is to candidly evaluate how much capacity currently exists to respond to these outside influences (Hamel and Prahalad, 1994; Prahalad and Hamel, 1990). Here, the answer to several key questions can be helpful. First, how well is the organization structured to respond to the needs of our customers? From the perspective of our customers, how easy are we to do business with? Where does responsibility for profitability lie in the organization? How well do departments work together? How effective are we at managing change (Barney, 1995)?

This evaluation may lead to the recognition that the firm is already stretched to near capacity. In this case, it would be unwise for the firm to attempt to take on more challenges until it has developed more internal capacity. On the other hand, some firms come out of this evaluation with the confidence that they can handle many additional challenges, and so they can become much more aggressive in pursuing opportunities in their target markets.

State the Annual Mission

Working with insights developed in the preceding analysis, members of the planning committee must next consolidate their learnings into a crisp mission statement that defines the geographical boundaries for the organization during the next year, the customer population to be served, what must be accomplished, and how these accomplishments will be measured. Here, the focus is on creating a balanced view that will take into consideration not only marketplace opportunities and threats but also what kind and how many initiatives can be successfully pursued by the firm given its current strengths and weaknesses.

LINKING STRATEGIC OBJECTIVES TO PROCESS IMPROVEMENTS

After the mission has been articulated, the next step is to translate this general statement into a set of specific, actionable goals for members throughout the organization. This is a vital step in the planning process, particularly if the quality message is to become part of the way that employees approach their work.

In identifying goals, organizations have recognized for a long time that it is important that they be specific, measurable, attainable, realistically high, and trackable. In addition, a system must be put in place to monitor progress being made toward the attainment of goals throughout the year. With such a system in place, feedback can be available throughout the year on how well the organization is doing, and interim steps can be taken when progress on key goals is not being realized. Then, at the end of the year, the overall results can be reviewed and provide valuable information for the next round of strategic planning. In this way, goal setting becomes a continuous process that helps the organization to learn more about its capacity for growth and renewal.

Balanced Scorecard Approach

What many organizations only started to discover in a formal way during the 1990s, however, is that another characteristic of goal setting can also significantly improve on the basic approach described earlier. This characteristic is to ensure that goals are also balanced.

More precisely, the emergence of the "balanced scorecard" approach, first described by Kaplan and Norton (1993, 1992), has proven to be a potent tool for conveying a richer picture of the strategy throughout the organization (Brenneman, 1998). How does this approach work? The fundamental premise of this tool is that traditional, short-term measures of success such as financial and operational results need to be complemented with long-term goals aimed at assessing customer satisfaction as well as organizational learning and development to provide a rounded strategy and approach to implementation.

The reason that this approach works is that traditional, short-term measures of success are "lagging" indicators of success. In other words, they are important, but they can tell you only where the organization has been, not where the organization is heading. In contrast, the long-term "leading" indicators of success let you make predictions about what is coming in the future (Kaplan and Atkinson, 1998; Rucci, Kirn, and Quinn, 1998). For example, when customer satisfaction ratings are going up, the future will be brighter. On the other hand, a decline in these measures is a sign of potential customer defections in the future (Reichheld and Sasser, 1990). Thus, when all four key categories are being measured, the focus of the organization is more balanced between meeting both short- and long-term objectives.

Other advantages to this approach are also worth noting. First, by applying relative weights to the four categories, it is possible for senior management to clearly indicate where the emphasis should be during the upcoming year, and the emphasis can change from year to year. For example, if cash flow is seen as a likely problem for the upcoming year, then the weight in the financial category can be increased. On the other hand, if a major new information system will be installed during the year, it might be advisable to increase the weight on the operational side of the equation. Naturally, increasing weights in any category means that the weights in the other categories need to be decreased to preserve an overall balance. In this way priorities are made clearer for everyone each year (Figure 4.1).

Second, this approach lends itself nicely to the design of performance management plans. Specifically, while the senior management team must set the high-level priorities, knowledge of these priorities allows departments, teams, and individuals to develop their own goals based on the larger strategic priorities of the organization (Meyer, 1994). Ideally, when the system is first being introduced, a cascading approach will be used. In other words, senior management should be the first group to begin using the process. Once it is familiar with how the system works, then it can serve as mentor and coach to the next level and so forth until the whole firm is using the system.

Third, using the balanced scorecard approach will not necessarily create more administrative work for the organization. Rather, it can be used to modify and even enhance existing performance management systems. See the Connecticut Renaissance case study in Chapter 8 for a more detailed description of how this can happen.

Finally, when everyone knows that he or she must contribute in some way to the attainment of goals in all four categories, it becomes clear that everyone's fate becomes linked to the overall success of the organization. In this way, a systemic, as opposed to individualistic, view of the organization is encouraged and rewarded (Deming, 1986).

Figure 4.1
Balanced Scorecard Approach to Goal Setting

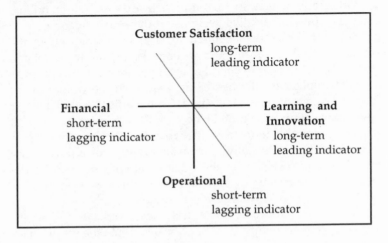

Develop a Goal/Process Matrix

The final step in an effective strategic planning process is to identify the set of critical, important, or broken processes from throughout the whole organization that must be improved to achieve the stated goals. This step is critical because while people can be developed to do their jobs better, individual best efforts are nonetheless limited by the type of systems that are in place (Juran, 1988; Deming, 1986; Crosby, 1979). Moreover, improving systems has the added value of also enhancing the performance of employees.

This last step in the planning process consists of five steps. First, all the organizational goals are posted. Then, for each goal, processes are identified that will have a definite impact on how likely it will be to achieve the goal. This analysis can be summarized in a two-by-two matrix. Step 3 is to rate the current status of each of the processes identified in step 2. A typical scale runs from 5 (excellent), to 4 (good), to 3 (average), to 2 (poor), to 1 (embryonic). Working with this information, it is possible in step 4 to determine both the current status (e.g., embryonic) of any given process and the number of goals (e.g., 3) that it will impact. The final step is to array the process status/number of goal(s) impacted data on a summary chart. Then, those processes most in need of improvement that also impact the largest number of goals are selected as targets for process improvement. During the course of the year, the target processes should ideally be improved sufficiently that they drop off the chart in future years, and so the cycle of continuous process improvement continues on from year to year (Hardaker and Ward, 1987).

In summary, as discussed at the outset of this chapter, there are many ways to think about strategic planning and its role in making a firm more successful this year and for years to come. So, how do you know if the strategic planning process has been successful in enhancing the quality of the firm? There are several suggestive measures that you may want to consider. Naturally, the first measure is the degree to which the target goals and objectives were met. Beyond that, it is important to ask, To what degree were the views of key stakeholders (e.g., customers, suppliers, employees) incorporated into the decision-making process? Third, to what degree could the process be described as part of an ongoing learning process? Fourth, was the plan widely understood throughout the organization? Fifth, did the planning effort lead to the improvement of critical processes? Finally, were adequate and appropriate rewards and recognition given to individuals who helped to make good things happen? Obviously, this list can be expanded. Yet, it is clear that as the ratings on each of these questions become more affirmative, you can rest assured that quality is settling more deeply into the fabric and culture of your firm.

REFERENCES

Argyris, C. 1994. Good communication that blocks learning. *Harvard Business Review*, 72 (4): 77–85.

Barney, J. 1995. Looking inside for competitive advantage. *Academy of Management Executive*, 9 (4): 49–61.

Bower, J. L., Bartlett, C. A., Uyterhoeven, H. E. R. & Walton, R. E. 1995. *Business policy: Managing strategic processes*. 8th ed. Chicago: Irwin.

Brenneman, G. 1998. Right away and all at once: How we saved
    Continental. *Harvard Business Review*, 76 (5): 162–179.

Cole, R. E., Bacdayan, P. & White, B. J. 1993. Quality, participation,
    and competitiveness. *California Management Review*, 35 (3): 68–
    81.

Collins, J. C., & Porras, J. I. 1996. Building your company's vision. *Harvard
    Business Review*, 74 (5): 65–77.

Collins , J. C., & Porras, J. I. 1994. *Built to last: Successful practices of
    visionary companies*. New York: Harper Business.

Crosby, P. B. 1979. *Quality is free: The art of making quality certain*. New
    York: McGraw-Hill.

de Geus, A. P. 1997. The living company. *Harvard Business Review*, 75 (2):
    51–59.

de Geus, A. P. 1988. Planning as learning. *Harvard Business Review*, 66
    (2):   70–74.

Deming, W. E. 1986. *Out of the crisis*. Cambridge: MIT Center for
    Advanced Engineering Study.

Drucker, P. 1994. The theory of the business. *Harvard Business Review*, 72
    (5): 95–104.

Finkelstein, S., & Hambrick, D. C. 1996. *Strategic leadership: Top
    executives and their effects on organizations*. Minneapolis: West.

Galbraith, J. R., Lawler, E. E. III & Associates 1993. *Organizing for the
    future: The new logic for managing complex organizations*. San
    Francisco: Jossey-Bass.

Garvin, D. A. 1987. Competing on the eight dimensions of quality.
    Harvard Business Review, 65 (6): 101–109.

Hambrick, D. C. & Mason, P. A. 1984. Upper echelons: The organiza-
    zation as a reflection of its top managers. *Academy of
    Management Review*, 9 (2): 193–206.

Hamel, G., & Prahalad, C. K. 1994. *Competing for the future*. Boston:
    Harvard Business School Press.

Hardaker, M., & Ward, B. K. 1987. How to make a team work. *Harvard
    Business Review*, 65 (6): 112–117.

Hax, A. C., & Majluf, N. S. 1991. *The strategy concept and process: A
    pragmatic approach*. Englewood Cliffs, NJ: Prentice-Hall.

Juran, J. M. 1988. *Juran on planning for quality*. New York: Free Press.

Kanter, R. M. 1994. Collaborative advantage: The art of alliances. *Harvard
    Business Review*, 72 (4): 96–108.

Kanter, R. M. 1989. Becoming PALs: Pooling, allying, and linking
    across companies. *Academy of Management Executive*, 3 (3): 183–
    193.

Kaplan, R. S., & Atkinson, A. A. 1998. *Advanced management accounting*. 3rd ed. Upper Saddle River, NJ: Prentice-Hall.

Kaplan, R. S., & Norton, D. P. 1993. Putting the balanced scorecard to work. *Harvard Business Review*, 71 (5): 134–147.

Kaplan, R. S., & Norton, D. P. 1992. The balanced scorecard: Measures that drive performance. *Harvard Business Review*, 70 (1): 71–79.

Levering, R., & Moskowitz, M. 2000. The 100 best companies to work for. *Fortune*, January 10: 82–84, 88, 90, 92, 96, 98, 102, 104, 109–110.

Meyer, C. 1994. How the right measures help teams excel. *Harvard Business Review*, 72 (3): 95–103.

Mintzberg, H. 1994. The fall and rise of strategic planning. *Harvard Business Review*, 72 (1): 107–114.

Mohrman, S. A., Cohen, S. G. & Mohrman, A. M., Jr. 1995. *Designing team-based organizations: New forms for knowledge work*. San Francisco: Jossey-Bass.

Nanus, B. 1992. *Visionary leadership*. San Francisco: Jossey-Bass.

Pine, B. J. II, & Gilmore, J. H. 1998. Welcome to the experience economy. *Harvard Business Review*, 76 (4): 97–105.

Porter, M. E. 1996. What is strategy? *Harvard Business Review*, 74 (6): 61–78.

Porter, M. E. 1985. *Competitive advantage: Creating and sustaining superior performance*. New York: Free Press.

Porter, M. E. 1980. *Competitive strategy: Techniques for analyzing industries and competitors*. New York: Free Press.

Prahalad, C. K., & Hamel, G. 1990. The core competence of the corporation. *Harvard Business Review*, 68 (3): 79–91.

Reichheld, F. F., & Sasser, W. E., Jr. 1990. Zero defections: Quality comes to services. *Harvard Business Review*, 68 (5): 105–111.

Rucci, A. J., Kirn, S. P. & Quinn, R. T. 1998. The employee-customer profit chain at Sears. *Harvard Business Review*, 76 (1): 82–97.

Sethia, N. K., & Von Glinow, M. A. 1985. Arriving at four cultures by managing the reward systems. In Kilmann, R. H., Saxton, M. J., Serpa, R. & Associates (Eds.), *Gaining control of the corporate culture*. 400–420. San Francisco: Jossey-Bass.

Treacy, M., & Wiersema, F. 1993. Customer intimacy and other value disciplines. *Harvard Business Review*, 71 (1): 84–93.

Chapter 5

Sharpening Customer Focus

If you don't know which way you want to go any road
is as good as any other.

—Cheshire Cat
Alice in Wonderland

One of the great strengths of quality organizations is that they are customer-focused. To achieve this goal, it is critical to become deeply aware of what your customers want and need. However, becoming customer-focused also means that you must make some tough choices. You will not be able to serve all people, even if they want to buy your products or services. Moreover, you will not be able to provide the same level of quality to all of the customers with whom you decide to do business. While this advice might sound like strong medicine to swallow, in this chapter we explore why it is nonetheless central to becoming recognized as a quality firm.

LISTENING TO THE VOICE OF THE CUSTOMER

As we discussed earlier, listening to the voice of the customer may not make life easy, but as many firms such as Xerox, USAA, Pepsi, and SmithKline Beecham have discovered, it may be the only way to ensure that you are still in business over the long term (Garvin, 1995). The first step in becoming a customer-focused organization, therefore, is to decide as a firm to begin actively listening to the voice of the customer in a *systematic* fashion. This advice may sound simple, but the reality is that most companies often face at least three related problems in making this transition.

Three Fundamental Problems

The first problem is that many organizations incorrectly assume that they are listening to the voice of the customer, when in fact they are not or are doing so poorly (Pine, Peppers, and Rogers, 1995). A sign that this may be occurring is the firm's knowing that it is losing market share, but no one really knows why this is happening. However, because this assumption is not challenged, the firm believes that it is in touch with its customers, and so no proactive steps are taken to improve the listening process (Argyris, 1993). As a consequence, the question of how well a firm is listening to its customers becomes a nonissue, and so no progress gets made on this important agenda (Argyris, 1994).

Another fundamental problem is that while many organizations do collect some data on customers, the data are not gathered into a central area where they can be analyzed and converted into actionable information for broad use throughout the firm, or the data are analyzed, but the results are never communicated throughout the organization.

The third fundamental problem stems from the interaction of the first two problems. Specifically, the quality of the data collection and analysis effort itself is not rigorously evaluated in a systematic fashion. In other words, the firm does not periodically examine what type of information is most important to gather to gain a deeper understanding of current and emerging customer preferences in particular, as well as market trends in general. As a result, the organization may simultaneously suffer from data overload and a lack of actionable information. When these conditions prevail, an organization may be forced to rely on "educated hunches" when making decisions about what customers really want, and this is always a risky approach to business.

Benefits from Active Listening

To illustrate why actively listening to your customers can be valuable for a firm, consider the following story detailed by Deming (1986). A large shipbuilding firm wanted to improve its process for planning and implementing ship-launching ceremonies. The firm's objective in undertaking this task was to improve relations with vendors and government agencies. So, the firm made a concerted effort to improve the way that it organized these events. After a while, it became very proficient at this task, so proficient, in fact, that it could host a major party every month as opposed to just once a year, and because it was so skillful at this activity, it decided that this was a good thing to do.

The fundamental flaw in the firm's approach, however, was failing to recognize that most of the suppliers and government officials did not want to go to this type of party every month. Indeed, after a while it became a burden and a bore for them to attend. Fortunately, by actively listening to feedback from its customers, the company came to recognize the error in its thinking. Specifically, while it could provide a very good service, its customers did not want it. Once it realized what had happened, it appropriately altered the format of the event such that the monthly events included only a select group of highly interested attendees. This change in venue led to better public relations (i.e., attaining the original goal) and reduced the cost of hosting the events for the shipbuilder. Everyone was happier.

CLARIFYING CUSTOMER SERVICE EXPECTATIONS

Most employees have good intentions and want to provide good service to their customers. However, what "doing a good job" means in everyday terms is not always clear to all employees. In other words, an employee may do what he or she thinks is best for a customer based on previous experience in similar situations or, in the absence of prior experience, on his or her best guess about how to handle the situation. Unfortunately, the employee's interpretation of the situation may not always be correct in the eyes of the company. Typically, the reason for this difference in opinion is that, based on internal priorities and past experience with customers, their organization prefers to approach the task in a different way.

Management Must Set Customer Service Standards

Setting standards for, and controlling variation in, customer service are not, however, the responsibility of employees. That job falls squarely on the shoulders of management. In other words, when an employee *unintentionally* mistreats a customer, it is not the employee's fault. It is the fault of management for failing to clarify its implicit expectations for how those interactions should unfold. Naturally, this is not the same as when an employee intentionally mishandles a customer. In that case, the employee and management need to work out a resolution, namely, that some behaviors are just unacceptable and will not be tolerated.

To ensure that appropriate levels of customer service are being provided, therefore, at a minimum, management must find a simple and effective way to convey its expectations to employees. A good illustration of how this can be done was seen in SAS Airlines. When Jan Carlson became president of this company, he coined a wonderful phrase for how the firm's employees should think about customer interactions. He described each of these customer interactions as a "moment of truth."

By this phrase, he sought to make clear to employees throughout the company that in the eyes of their customers *they are the company*. From this perspective, every customer interaction, which includes individuals inside as well as outside the organization, represents the opportunity to make a good or bad impression. Over time, these moments of truth add up to convey an image of what quality standards are operating within the company (Pine and Gilmore, 1998).

What Is Our Value Proposition?

To provide truly excellent customer service, however, employees must also know the answer to several fundamental questions that only senior management can provide. First, whom do we want to serve? Second, what needs do these customers have? Third, what are we willing to offer to our customers? By answering these questions, the firm clarifies what has been called a "value proposition" that needs to be widely understood throughout the organization. Indeed, market leading firms are frequently organized around a single, clearly recognized value proposition.

More precisely, while quality organizations understand that enhancing customer satisfaction must be one of their primary goals, they also know that there are many ways to pursue this objective. In addition, they know that customers likewise seek different kinds of value from their suppliers depending on what product or service is being purchased.

For example, some purchases will be determined on the basis of low cost and ease of delivery. Other purchases will go to the supplier who can provide the most customized and tailored goods or services. Meanwhile, other deals will be made with whoever can provide a unique solution to a special need (Treacy and Wiersema, 1995, 1993).

In studying how leading firms address this reality, Treacy and Wiersema (1995, 1993) discovered some interesting patterns. First, market leaders consistently provide threshold value around all three propositions, which they called "operational excellence," "customer intimacy," and "innovation," respectively, but these firms also clearly excelled and built their reputation in one area. At the same time, they discovered that when firms attempt to excel in all three, as Sears did briefly in the late 1980s and early 1990s, they will meet with disaster. In other words, you will not succeed if you try to be all things to all people.

All Customers Are Not Equal

When you accept that, depending on what is being bought, purchasers will be seeking different values from their suppliers, it becomes clear from a supplier's perspective that all customers are not equal. Only those customers who are seeking the kind of value that your firm can deliver should be actively pursued because these customers will most likely be delighted with the experience.

This logic can be scary for firms that have been opportunistic as opposed to strategic in their growth and development. Yet, the best way to ensure the long-term viability of a firm is to build loyalty with customers who like what you have to offer and let the others go to someone else. The best way to build this loyalty is to develop rich channels of communication between yourself and your customers and, most importantly, when customers complain, to listen carefully to their concerns and *take action* to make things better (Hart, Heskett, and Sasser, 1990).

In other words, the best relationships are built on clear expectations. Therefore, in every communication with current and potential customers, suppliers must be as clear as possible about the level of quality that they will be able to provide. This message establishes baseline expectations in the mind of the customer for what to anticipate from involvement in the relationship. In this way, different products such as a Toyota and a Mercedes-Benz can both be viewed as high-quality automobiles, just different.

Thus, in a world where only a passion for, and commitment to, delighting customers will win the day, it may be necessary for a firm to rethink its relationship with current and potential customers. Specifically, in the past firms knew that meeting the growing demands of customers would be a daunting task. Now, it is becoming more evident that trying to meet the needs of everyone who is potentially interested in purchasing your products or services is an impossible task. Therefore, to be a quality organization, firms must become clear about whom they want to serve, whom they might serve, and whom they will not serve.

GAINING DEEPER KNOWLEDGE OF THE CUSTOMER

Deciding whom to serve and in what manner is a critical and challenging task. No one wants to make any mistakes in this arena. If you are committed to systematically gaining a deeper understanding of your customers, however, it is possible to make more informed choices. There are a number traditional ways that this task has been approached, such as through the use of standardized customer satisfaction surveys (Hayes, 1992), running focus groups (Krueger, 1994), and conducting customer visits (McQuarrie, 1993), that have proven to be useful in gaining richer insights into customers' perceptions of the level of quality that they are receiving from suppliers (McQuarrie, 1996; Klein, Masi, and Weidner, 1995). Several more refined methods for generating actionable information about customers are emerging, however, that also warrant serious consideration. Three of these representative approaches are described next.

Whom Do We Want to Serve?

Many organizations have mistaken ideas about who their "best" customers are because they look only at the surface of their business relationship. Specifically, the value of a customer cannot be determined by looking only at the volume of business that he or she generates. That is, large-volume customers are great, medium-volume customers are good, small-volume customers are bad. Only a careful look at the cost of mix of transactions (e.g., size of orders, delivery costs) typically involved in each relationship, combined with an accurate measure of the total benefits (e.g., profit margins, number of referrals) associated with each type of transaction can answer this cost-benefit question.

One of the most useful tools to emerge on the quality front during the last decade to help answer this cost-benefit question comes from the field of accounting. This methodology is called activity-based costing (ABC) (Kaplan and Atkinson, 1998). In a distinct break from more traditional accounting approaches aimed at counting things, this approach also looks closely at all the activities involved in completing a transaction to determine the actual costs and benefits associated with it. This process-oriented approach can shed considerable light on how much it actually costs to serve a client by revealing both the true total costs and overall benefits to be derived from the relationship. Thus, by examining what types of transactions different customers are involved in, it is possible to obtain a more accurate picture of exactly how profitable various customers are for the firm.

What Are Our Customers' Real Needs?

How do you know when you have satisfied your customers' needs? The traditional approach is to create a uniform customer satisfaction survey based on well-recognized evaluation criteria. Certainly this approach is convenient for the supplier and consistent across customers, which makes comparisons across customers relatively easy for the supplier.

Yet, there is a potential weakness in this approach. Specifically, if everyone receives the same questionnaire, then how good is the information received? Clearly, if all customers have exactly the same needs, there is little to worry about with this approach. On the other hand, if customers have different needs, this one-size-fits-all approach can be very misleading because aggregate numbers often mask important stories buried deep in the details.

Assuming that considerable variation does, in fact, exist across customers, a better approach is to allow customers to become involved in creating their own customer satisfaction measures and thereby help to clarify for the supplier what value they are actually seeking from the relationship. This end is easily achieved by merely allowing customers to select the questions to which they want to respond from a carefully refined list of questions. This approach has two great advantages. One advantage is that the customer feels more involved in the evaluation process and is therefore more likely both to complete the questionnaire and to give it more serious thought. The other major advantage is that by picking the questions to answer, the customer is, in fact, defining his or her own current and evolving "value propositions." Armed with this information, the supplier can make more informed judgments about whether or not the customer's needs make them more or less attractive as customers going forward.

What Do Our Customers Really Want?

An associated issue is determining what customers actually want from their suppliers. A traditional way for suppliers to get at this issue is through a win-loss analysis where winning and losing proposals are closely examined to determine what combination of offerings led them to be selected or rejected by a customer. Then, based on a cost-benefit analysis, the supplier can determine if the cost to the firm is worth the benefits derived from the relationship with the customer.

Recently, some firms have taken this form of analysis to a higher level by asking more customer-focused questions. For example, if a customer did not select us because of cost, is he or she willing to accept substitute products or services that we can offer at lower prices? If this alternative is not acceptable, is there a way for us to redesign our products and services such that they offer greater value at lower cost? Third, is there a way for us to streamline our processes and operations to reduce the activity costs associated with providing our products and services (Kaplan and Atkinson, 1998)?

Another promising approach is to look not just at individual contracts but at the entire profit model that organizes the way that a firm will do business with its customers to discover deeper sources of competitive advantage (Slywotzky and Morrison, 1997). The most notable example here is Sears. After hitting very rough financial times in the early 1990s, the company decided to step back and look at the basic model that was guiding its business. What it discovered was that the old model of trying to offer operational excellence, customer intimacy, and innovative products and services at the same time and in the same building was not working. Accordingly, it set out to create a new model.

The result was the development of a new, integrated profit model that identified the relationships that connected employee satisfaction, customer satisfaction, and investor satisfaction in a seamless chain. To move forward, the company concluded that the answer was to make Sears a compelling place to work, shop, and invest. This model proved to be so powerful that not only did profits improve dramatically, but the firm was able to predict with considerable accuracy how improvements in employee satisfaction would lead to subsequent enhancements in customer satisfaction and overall firm results (Rucci, Kirn, and Quinn, 1998).

A CLOSER LOOK: FIDELITY INVESTMENTS

Fidelity Investments was founded in 1946 by Edward C. Johnson II on a philosophy of continuous improvement. At its founding, the basic working premise of the firm was to work harder and smarter every day to help a small group of investors meet their financial goals. Today, this Boston-based investment giant manages over $856 billion in mutual funds for 15 million investors (Smith, 1999)!

There are many reasons behind the phenomenal success of this firm over the years. One consistent factor, however, is that the company has always been sensitive to changing investment patterns and the evolving needs of its customers. It is not surprising, therefore, that with the rapid growth of retirement assets from $8.1 trillion to $10 trillion between 1996 and 1998, Fidelity was busy making plans for how it could become more helpful to its clients in making decisions in this area.

Clearly, a firm like Fidelity could be helpful to investors with their retirement concerns in a number of beneficial ways. One way is to offer investment vehicles as part of a employer's defined benefits plan. The second way is to provide employees with a variety of ways to invest in a defined contribution or 401K plan. Third, any eligible individual could also use the vast array of Fidelity's investment options to fund his or her personal IRA.

In 1996, however, the Retirement Services Group within the firm decided that it needed to get closer to its customers. It needed to learn more precisely what was going on in the lives of its investors, so it could more richly understand the role that retirement funding decisions were playing in their overall life planning process.

To develop this deeper understanding, it conducted a series of targeted marketed studies. It discovered from these studies three important pieces of information. First, the average age of its investors placed them closer to potential retirement than most of the general population. Second, these individuals had larger balances than the national average. Third, they were moving from job to job more frequently than the average employee.

As it probed more deeply, it found that in terms of retirement, its investors were primarily concerned with three issues that revolved around changing lifestyles. What would they do when they finally decided to retire? How would they create a budget to live on after retirement? What kind of investment strategy should they pursue in retirement?

The biggest question on the minds of its investors, therefore, was whether or not they had enough money to retire and live comfortably in the future. But the answer to this question was made more complex by the fact that most of these individuals knew that people were living longer. They were not completely sure how much money they would need to live on. They had some flexibility in determining when they would actually decide to retire, and they might even decide to take on one or more new jobs before they made the transition to full retirement.

For its part, Fidelity knew some things that most investors do not know. For example, when it comes to changing jobs, in particular, many investors did not always make the best decisions about how to take their retirement assets with them. Specifically, based on data from a 1998 Employee Benefits Research Institute study, in 1997 only 48% of workers preserved *all* their retirement benefits when changing jobs. Most of this "loss" was due to the payment of taxes that could have been avoided (Slear, 1999). In addition, Fidelity knew that when retirement funds are transferred from one employer benefit program to another, on average only between 22% and 28% of the funds will remain with the same investment company.

In these sobering statistics Fidelity saw a great opportunity. If it could somehow take the lead on educating investors on how to make the most informed investment decisions, then it could help itself by helping others. Its answer to this challenge was to put together a seasoned team of investment specialists to educate people on-site at companies as well as have dedicated retirement consultants available in the Investor Centers or by telephone. Since 1998, Fidelity Investments has offered these seminars to almost 30,000 individuals, its dual goals in doing so being to increase its current customer base and to experience a threefold increase in the percentage of funds being retained by the company when an individual does decide to change employers. It is well on the way to meeting both goals.

In summary, one of the most critical challenges facing every organization is to become truly customer-focused. This means not only listening to customers' needs, but, more importantly, deciding with whom you will and will not do business based on the kind of value that your firm can offer to current and potential customers. Fortunately, new tools and techniques are emerging to make this decision-making process more effective. Nonetheless, the real challenge is to be able to make the hard calls and then driving this vision deep into the organization's business and work processes.

REFERENCES

Argyris, C. 1994. Good communication that blocks learning. *Harvard Business Review*, 72 (4): 77–85.

Argyris, C. 1993. *Knowledge for action*. San Francisco: Jossey-Bass.

Deming, W. E. 1986. *Out of the crisis*. Cambridge: MIT Center for Advanced Engineering Study.

Garvin, D. A. 1995. Leveraging processes for strategic advantage: A roundtable with Xerox's Allaire, USAA's Herres, SmithKline Beecham's Leschly, and Pepsi's Weatherup. *Harvard Business Review*, 73 (5): 76–90.

Hart, C. W. L., Heskett, J. L. & Sasser, W. E., Jr. 1990. The profitable art of service recovery. *Harvard Business Review*, 68 (4): 148–156.

Hayes, B. E. 1992. *Measuring customer satisfaction: Development and use of questionnaires*. Milwaukee, WI: ASQC Quality Press.

Kaplan, R. S., & Atkinson, A. A. 1998. *Advanced management accounting*. 3rd ed. Upper Saddle River, NJ: Prentice-Hall.

Klein, A. S., Masi, R. J. & Weidner, C. K. II 1995. Organization culture, distribution and amount of control, and perceptions of quality. *Group & Organization Management,* 20 (2): 122–148.

Krueger, R. A. 1994. *Focus groups: A practical guide for applied research.* 2nd ed. Thousand Oaks, CA: Sage.

McQuarrie, E. F. 1996. *The market research toolbox: A concise guide for beginners.* Thousand Oaks, CA: Sage.

McQuarrie, E. F. 1993. *Customer visits: Building a better market focus.* Newbury Park, CA: Sage.

Pine, J. B. II, & Gilmore, J. H. 1998. Welcome to the experience economy. *Harvard Business Review,* 76 (4): 97–105.

Pine, J. B. II, Peppers, D. & Rogers, M. 1995. Do you want to keep your customers forever? *Harvard Business Review,* 73 (2): 36–47.

Rucci, A. J., Kirn, S. P. & Quinn, R. T. 1998. The employee-customer profit chain at Sears. *Harvard Business Review,* 76 (1): 82–97.

Slear, T. 1999. Changing jobs, facing choices. *Fidelity Focus,* Winter: 18–21.

Slywotzky, A. J., & Morrison, D. J. 1997. *The profit zone: How strategic business design will lead you to tomorrow's profits.* New York: Random House.

Smith, G. 1999. Fidelity.com gets serious. *Business Week,* July 19: 84.

Treacy, M., & Wiersema, F. 1995. *The discipline of market leaders.* Reading, MA: Addison-Wesley.

Treacy, M., & Wiersema, F. 1993. Customer intimacy and other value disciplines. *Harvard Business Review,* 71 (1): 84–93.

Chapter 6

Organizing a Process Improvement Effort

The timid and the fainthearted, and people who expect quick results, are doomed to disappointment.

—W. Edwards Deming, 1986

As discussed at the outset of this book, making a commitment to continuous improvement as a way of life for an organization will not necessarily increase this quarter's dividends. On the other hand, as the "Baldrige Index" results show, long-term investors will benefit handsomely from this decision. The reason that a long-term view is necessary is that building a continuous improvement infrastructure and creating a supportive culture to make this new management approach take hold requires time, patience, persistence, and resources. Yet, the process for establishing a successful program is not that mysterious. Every successful organization will do it in a slightly different way, but the basic outline is clear. So, if you want a quick-fix solution to your business problems, don't look to process improvement for much help. If you are seeking a long-term investment where the payback will grow each year, however, there are few options better suited to your needs.

PROCESS LESSONS FROM EVERYDAY LIFE

Getting started on the quality journey can be a daunting endeavor until you recognize that every activity is a process. Once you see the ubiquity of processes, then everything else becomes relatively easy to understand. For instance, we can use the simple example of a daily commute to reveal some powerful lessons about how processes influence our life every day and how we can use knowledge of process management principles to make life better.

The first step in understanding process management is to accept the dictum that if you cannot or do not measure something, you do not really understand it. So, to begin understanding the nature of your daily commute as a process, we would start by asking the question, "How long does it take you to drive from home to work?" If your answer is, "I think it usually takes about 30 minutes," there are two things immediately troubling with your answer from a process management perspective. First, to improve a process, "thinking" is not sufficient. What you need to do is actually measure the time that it takes to complete the commute. Second, answers such as "about 30 minutes" are inadequate to describe the performance characteristics of a process. What you need to know is precisely how long the commute takes based on your experience over a number of days using exactly the same route. So, if you have not timed your commute on a regular basis with an accurate watch over the last few weeks, you cannot really answer this most basic process management question.

Let's assume that you decided to get serious about understanding your commute as a process that can be managed and improved. In this case, to get started, the first thing you would need to do is precisely measure how long the commute takes today. For the sake of this example, let's say you found that Monday's commute took exactly 30 minutes.

This is important information to have and the first step along the way to better managing the process. Once you know this information, it would need to be plotted on what in the world of statistical process control (SPC) is called a run chart for Monday (Figure 6.1). Next, you would need to keep track of all the commuting times for the remainder of the week and also plot these data points on your run chart.

Figure 6.1
Analysis of a Daily Commute

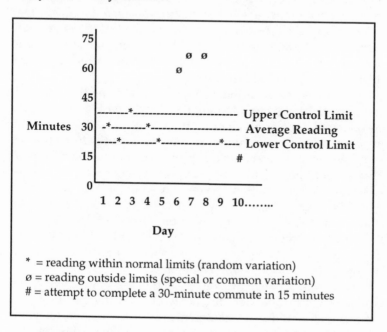

The great benefit of having these data is that they allow you to now use the power of some simple statistical tools to gain greater insight into the nature of the commute. For example, with these data, you can now calculate the average amount of time it takes you to commute each day. This information would also need to be plotted on your run chart (Figure 6.1). Then, again using these basic data, we could calculate what is called a standard deviation. A standard deviation is useful to know because it shows how much variation exists around the mean score. Note here that from a process management perspective, less variation around the mean is always better than more variation, so a small standard deviation is better than a large one. Working with this information about the naturally occurring variation within your commute, we can next proceed to set what are known as upper and lower control limits for "normal" acceptable variation during the commute. For the sake of this illustration, let's say our standard deviation turned out to be 5 minutes. With this knowledge, we could decide to set our upper and lower control limits at +/- 1 standard deviation. So, going forward, we would consider any commute that takes between 25 minutes (i.e., lower control limit) and 35 minutes (i.e., upper control limit) to be within an acceptable range of normal variation (Figure 6.1) or our established tolerable range of variation.

Continuing on with the example, let's assume that on your commute the following Monday (i.e., Day 6 on Figure 6.1) you encountered a major accident on the interstate highway leading to work, and so your commute took 60 minutes to complete. What should you do about your plans to commute the next day? This is a very important example of the type of process management question that surfaces every day in organizations, so it is worth exploring. Some folks would say that it would be best to change the travel route to be sure you do not get delayed again the next day. Others would say that it is best to do nothing, since the accident was probably just a random event and will not happen again at that location for a long time.

If you said "change the route," then in the language of process management you were implicitly or explicitly deciding that the accident would be a "common cause" of variation for your commute in the future. That is, the section of the road where the accident occurred was poorly designed (Taguchi and Clausing, 1990), so it could be anticipated that additional accidents would frequently occur there and thus would continually delay your commute. Given this view, your opinion of the adequacy of the current commuting process has been fundamentally changed, and you must do something about it. On the other hand, if you thought that the accident was just a random occurrence, then you have classified it as a "special cause" of variation. Accordingly, since you believe that the problem will be fixed in time for your commute the next day, you would not do anything about it. So, you would leave your house at exactly the same time the next day and use the same route.

Pushing on with the example, let us assume that you decided that Monday's delay was due to a fluke accident. On Tuesday (i.e., Day 7 on Figure 6.1) you left at the usual time, but during this commute you ran into a construction project being set up on your main route, which caused your commute to take 70 minutes. Being an optimist, you tried the same route the next day, and now the construction project looked even more permanent, and once again it took you 70 minutes to complete the drive. Well, if this construction project is like most on major highways, it will be a long time before you can enjoy the old 30-minute commute again. That is, due to a common cause of variation (i.e., the construction project) your commute along this route has been significantly altered. The commuting process that you have been using has been fundamentally changed, and until things return to preconstruction conditions, trying to make better time on this route is futile. So, find a way to change the commute by using another route, leaving earlier, and so on.

On Day 9 you do the logical thing and try another route to work. The result is great news. Using this new route and driving within the speed limit, it takes you only 25 minutes to get to work! It looks as if you have found another and maybe even better process for commuting to work.

Now, on to the last lesson to be drawn from this example. It is Friday of week 2 and you have overslept. Since you have an important meeting at work, you try to complete the commute in 15 minutes. What will happen? In all likelihood your attempt to speed up the commute to work will result in some bad news. You might get stopped by the police and receive a ticket, which will add time and expense to the commute. Worse yet, you might get into an accident, which will cost serious time, money, and personal pain.

Why doesn't the attempt to speed up the process work? The reason is that every process has natural performance limitations built into it. Any attempt to artificially speed up a process is doomed to failure. This is why attempts by managers to artificially speed up processes by promised incentives or threats often backfire. The only way to truly speed up a process is to change it.

SELECTING PROJECTS

As discussed in Chapters 4 and 5, the first two interrelated steps in establishing an effective quality improvement effort are to develop a broadly understood strategic quality orientation throughout the firm (Porter, 1996) that is aimed at delighting certain types of customers (Pine and Gilmore, 1998). Creating this foundation is necessary but not sufficient for the long-term success of the effort. To make continuous quality improvement a way of life for an organization, the engine that must be created is a formal process improvement program (Fairfield-Sonn, 1999).

The use of the word *program* here is important to emphasize, because experience has shown that isolated or informal efforts at process improvements typically yield marginal or fleeting improvements at best. The reason for this is simple. Process improvement is not a quick-fix strategy (Heifetz, 1994). To reap significant rewards from *work* process improvement efforts (Garvin, 1995), an organization must be committed to the long view and be focused on the highest-priority process improvement opportunities (Juran, 1988).

At the heart of any effective program, therefore, is the project selection process. Since the identification of the most important projects requires knowledge of the future direction of the firm based on an understanding of the current external opportunities and threats as well as internal strengths and weaknesses of the organization, this work must fall to the senior management team. Ideally, this will be a part of the annual strategic planning process.

More precisely, since the strategic planning process will lead to the identification of the organization's annual goals, in the context of these discussions it is relatively easy to drill the analysis down one more level to the identification of those key work processes that are either important, broken, or nonexistent and will have the greatest impact on the likelihood of the firm's attaining its goals.

It is important to recognize, however, that the logic for selecting process improvement targets is quite different from the logic for selecting the firm's goals. When you identify goals for a firm, the focus is on picking the most important areas to pursue that will lead to excellent performance. In contrast, the selection of process improvement opportunities is driven by the desire to identify those processes that impact the largest number of goals, and if left unattended, will do the most to inhibit organizational performance. In other words, if you rated processes on a five-point scale from embryonic (1), to poor (2), to average (3), to good (4), and to excellent (5), all things being equal, you would want to direct your attention at the processes with the lowest ratings. The reason for this decision-making rule is that even small improvements to poor processes will lead to significant performance gains, while improvements to highly rated processes will typically yield only marginal improvements.

Beyond the preceding "impact potential" decision rule, several other guidelines can be useful in selecting the best processes to attack (Scholtes, Joiner, and Streibel, 1996). For example, it is useful at the start of a program to address processes that directly impact external customers. Second, all managers concerned with the process should agree that it needs attention. Third, the process should not be currently being studied or changed by another group. Fourth, individuals involved with the process will cooperate in changing the process. Fifth, the process has easily identifiable starting and ending points, and the process occurs on a frequent basis so it will be easy to study and modify.

GETTING STARTED

As discussed earlier, to be successful, dedication to continuous process improvement must become a way of life within a firm, that is, a cultural imperative. When this happens, every member of the organization from the president to the newest employee understands not only the importance of process improvement as a key tool to enhancing the organization's productivity and competitiveness but also what role that he or she needs to play in contributing to this effort. This contribution may vary from a senior management team's selecting process improvement targets, to an individual's serving as a member of a team or implementing the process changes that are discovered over time (Fairfield-Sonn, 1999). In other words, there are many important, interrelated roles to play, and everyone throughout the organization must understand how he or she can contribute to the overall effort for it to be successful (Zack and McKenney, 1996).

Over time, every quality organization will invariably develop well-understood, company-specific structures and methodologies for how to go about the important work of improving internal processes (Bounds, 1996). This capacity, however, must be created, institutionalized, monitored, and reinforced for the program to become effective. Once a critical mass of employees comes to understand how the structures work and have mastered these methods, however, the organization has a potent tool to use in pursuing a variety of strategic goals. Indeed, process improvement teams can become one of the most powerful means available for addressing strategic goals (see Malcolm Baldrige Award winners in Chapter 3). Getting started itself requires that decisions be made and actions taken in several areas.

Coordination

The first major implementation issue that needs to be addressed is how and who will coordinate the overall effort. There are many ways to create these coordinating bodies, which are often called quality councils. In designing them, several criteria have proven to be beneficial. First, the coordinating team should be large enough to allow for fairly wide representation from key functional areas within the organization, but not so large as to make meetings a logistical nightmare. Anywhere between 6 and 12 members is usually an optimal target size. Second, individuals serving on the quality council should have a solid understanding of the strategic plan and why specific process improvement efforts are critical to the pursuit of the firm's major objectives. This understanding could come from serving on the strategic planning team or being briefed in sufficient detail by individuals directly involved in the effort such that the council members feel fully comfortable with the organization's strategic direction. Third, members of the coordination team should themselves be knowledgeable about the basic tools and techniques of process improvement. In other words, quality council members need to know where the organization is going and how to be helpful to the teams that are making this vision a reality. Yet, this should not be confused with micromanagement. In other words, council members should stay in touch with the teams so they can be helpful where and when needed, but ultimately the team must do the work itself.

Once members have been selected to serve on the quality council, which is often a rotational and developmental assignment, the next step in the program rollout is for the council itself to establish process improvement teams (PITs). Here again, a variety of approaches has been successfully used. Ultimately, the staffing and training decisions here ride on a few key questions. Three of these important decisions are highlighted next.

Staffing and Training

First, what role should the team leader play? Specifically, should the team leader be responsible for completing the assigned task and managing the group's processes, or will these responsibilities be divided between the team leader and a team facilitator?

Second, how many members should be formally assigned to any process improvement team? Here, experience has shown that the optimal size means having as few individuals as possible assigned to any given team while still ensuring that sufficient process content expertise is available within the group. This does not mean that all of the necessary expertise is available for the entire duration of the project. There will always be some individuals who have useful insights in particular aspects of the process but who are not involved in most of it. These individuals can advise the main team on an as-needed basis, but do not serve as team members per se. Following this staffing pattern will benefit the organization by making the best use of human resources. Moreover, the "advisers," in particular, will be more willing to become involved because they have to come to meetings only when they can make a real contribution.

Third, how much training on quality improvement tools and techniques should be provided to team leaders, team facilitators, where appropriate, and team members prior to starting their assignments? Experience has shown that of the three staffing and training questions to be addressed, perhaps the most important is what kind of training will be provided and to whom. One of three routes has typically been pursued. Some firms have decided that everyone involved in a PIT should be trained prior to participation on a team. Another popular option is to train only the team leader, who is often selected when these individuals will be responsible both for completing the assignment and for managing the team's work processes. The third option is to invest heavily in the training of team facilitators with the intent that they, in turn, will provide on-the-job training for the team leaders and the team members during the course of various projects.

Regardless of who is selected for training, some in-depth process improvement knowledge is critical to a PIT's success because there is a fairly clear and orderly process that all successful teams go through, and this process can be learned. On the other hand, if no one really understands this process, it is highly likely that the team will flounder along the way, become discouraged, and may never complete its work.

The reason that PITs can easily get lost in their effort is twofold. Part of the explanation lies in the fact that running a successful PIT requires well-developed interpersonal skills and understanding of a substantial body of technical knowledge. More precisely, to be effective, team leaders and/or team facilitators need to know how to work with a diverse group of individuals to mold them into a team that can bring a project to a successful closure while yielding individual, group, and organizational results and satisfaction. In addition, they need to have a broad knowledge base of continuous improvement that includes a general theoretical foundation about why quality improvement works and the stages involved in the effort. Moreover, from a statistical perspective they need knowledge of sampling techniques, control methodologies, and capability analysis.

The other part of the challenge comes from the fact that, unlike most other organizational assignments, these efforts often involve cross-functional participation from team members on a part-time basis. Accordingly, when significant challenges or potential roadblocks are encountered because of a lack of knowledge around process improvement tools and techniques, team members will often choose to devote more of their energies to their full-time job in their area of functional expertise at the expense of working on the PIT assignment.

This decision is not hard to understand. In most organizations completing functional assignments is where the major rewards come from. So, to make a PIT successful requires great facilitation skills on the part of the team leader and/or the team facilitator as well as the visible support of senior management through the quality council. Indeed, given this reality of organizational life, it is not hard to see why facilitation skills very often even outrank task skills in determining the ultimate level of success experienced by a PIT.

Reporting Relationships

As PITs are being staffed and deployed, the quality council must also decide on what type of reporting relationships will be most effective to provide ongoing guidance without undue control. Many methods of reporting team progress have also been used, and these often reflect the culture of the organization at the time of the program launch. For example, Fairfield-Sonn (1999) reported on three different approaches that he observed, namely, a hierarchical or bureaucratic approach, a coordinating approach, and a sponsor approach. In the hierarchical approach, the team leaders provided formal monthly progress reports to the quality council. In the coordinating model, the PITs worked in an ongoing collegial relationship with the quality council to complete their analysis. In other words, the quality council served as a resource to the team and helped it think through any problems that it encountered. The third approach was labeled sponsorship, because the senior officers in the firm acted as sounding boards for the ongoing work of the process improvement teams. In this way the sponsors could help the team think through issues as they emerged and even run interference for foreseeable future problems.

Determining End Points

Another important issue for the quality council to consider is how they will determine when a team's work is done. This may seem like a simple issue, but it will be recalled that this was a central issue in the debate between Deming and Juran. Deming advocated that all processes should be constantly improved. Juran argued that a process should be improved only to the point where the benefits exceeded the costs. At that point, the process improvement effort should be stopped.

As a matter of practice, Fairfield-Sonn (1999) observed a number of ways that this issue was resolved. In one firm, the process was improved to the point where a target goal of improvement had been reached, however long it took. Once this level of success had been reached, the PIT was disbanded. In another organization, improvement in the process was aimed at making the greatest improvement possible. This end point was determined through ongoing dialogue between the team and the quality council. Another firm created a time-based model, where the PIT made the greatest improvements that it could within tightly prescribed time limits. When time ran out, the PIT's work was considered to be done.

CONDUCTING THE ANALYSIS

The broad outline for how to improve a process is surprisingly simple in design, but there can be enormous complexity in the execution of each major step along the way (Scholtes, Joiner, and Streibel, 1996). Therefore, in many ways agreeing to work on a PIT is like signing up to take a trip through a long, dimly lighted mountain tunnel that will hopefully lead to a happy valley on the other side. Naturally, the thought of this journey can provoke anxiety in many would-be travelers, and for good cause. Many teams, particularly those that attempt the first trip without the benefit of a seasoned guide, become lost and disoriented in the tunnel for a long time. In the worst case, they decide to abandon the effort and return to the tunnel entrance. On the other hand, veterans of the journey will tell you that it can be one of the most challenging and fun assignments that you can have to work on because, while each trip will be slightly different, by following a few simple signposts along the way, the journey always ends up well. Next, each of the four major phases of a process improvement effort is briefly described.

Look Inside

The first step in a process improvement effort is to look inside your own internal operations to determine how well you are currently handling a process. To do this effectively, it is critical to begin by being very clear about the team's mission. Specifically, two issues must be precisely understood. One issue that must be crystal-clear concerns the scope of the process improvement effort. In other words, where does the process on interest begin and end? These are often called the process bookends. The second key component of the mission is understanding what the objectives of the effort are aimed at accomplishing. These are best framed in terms of customer requirements. For example, requirements can range from decreasing the time to delivery, to improving the accuracy of delivery, to improving the style of delivery, and so on.

Given a clear understanding of the scope of the project, the next step in the improvement process is to develop a detailed flowchart of the process as it currently exists. In other words, a map must be created that shows every key step in the sequential process that leads to the final outcome. To create this map, two guidelines must be followed. First, in building this map the PIT needs to interview the individuals doing the work as opposed to merely outlining how they think that the work is currently being done. Second, during these interviews the PIT members must stress to the interviewees that they need to explain how it is currently being done and not how it should be done.

After this map is created, it is often easy for the PIT to spot some obvious areas where the process is probably breaking down. Some red flags are steps that lead to significant delays, steps that are unnecessarily complex, and steps where there is wide reported variation in how the work is done. Noting these steps can lead to some immediate ideas on how to enhance the process.

Before making any recommendations, however, the PIT needs to confirm or disconfirm its hunches with the folks who are actually doing the work. One highly effective way to do this is to invite the individuals who do the work to review the entire map and pick the three areas where the process most often breaks down. With this information the PIT can construct what is called a Pareto Chart. This chart is a simple graphical representation of what steps lead to the greatest number of problems in the process. This charting procedure is powerful because it allows the PIT to easily summarize the trouble spots from most frequent to least frequent in occurrence. Moreover, it takes advantage of a powerful behavioral principle first discovered and demonstrated by Pareto, an Italian sociologist, that 80% of most problems can be traced back to 20% of the reasons for the observed effect. For example, 80% of most managers' problems can be traced back to the attitudes and behaviors of 20% of their employees.

Once the most troubling steps in the process have been identified, the next step in the analysis is to drill down one more level to get at the root cause(s) of the problem. Insight into the deeper causes is often gained through the use of what is called a fishbone or root-cause analysis. To conduct this analysis, each troubling step is closely inspected to determine what is leading to the difficulties in executing the step. Common areas of potential concern are the production methods being used, the instruments being used to measure quality both during the process and after the final product or service is created, the physical environment, the machines used in the process, the materials being used in the process, and the qualifications, skills, and attitudes of the employees doing the work.

Look Outside

After the root-cause analysis has been completed, the PIT is now in a good position to begin cleaning up obvious problems in the process. At this point, the PIT can start to work on the second phase of the process improvement effort, which is to look outside the organization for some potential solutions to the most difficult process-related problems. It should be noted that in many organizations this step constitutes an important cultural shift. It requires moving from assuming that the solutions to all problems lie within the organization, to taking the view that some other really smart organizations may have already looked at the same issue and come up with some innovative solutions that could speed up the PIT's learning process.

There are many ways to look outside an organization for some potentially useful ideas. For example, it is easy to start by reviewing industry and academic publications for articles related to the issues of concern. Another useful starting place is to attend conferences on topics of interest to the firm. At some point, however, the PIT will need to begin making direct contact with a select group of companies to conduct personal interviews with company representatives about the nature of their concerns and how the target firms have addressed these issues. This process is called "benchmarking."

Benchmarking is both a science and an art (Camp 1995, 1989). To be successful in this venture, a few simple rules need to be followed (Main, 1992; Port and Smith, 1992). First, before you attempt to benchmark with another firm, do your homework. In other words, you need to know everything possible about your own internal processes and the ways that others have addressed them before you make the call. The call should be a well-thought-through attempt to get at some targeted information about a process. That is, benchmarking works best when it is viewed as a targeted rifle shot rather than a shotgun approach. If you are well prepared, the entire interview should take no more than 15 minutes to complete.

Second, you should be prepared to share information with your benchmarking partner. There are two dimensions to this sharing. One dimension is that you should never ask a question of someone else that you are not prepared to answer in complete candor with the interviewee. The other dimension is that most folks are willing to benchmark with you if there is something they can get in return. Typically, that something is information that they might be able to use to improve their own processes. So, often the price of playing is to provide the benchmark partner with a copy of your final report. Third, you must respect the needs for confidentiality that your partner might have. Accordingly, if a partner says that some information is not for public consumption, that is what it means. Often this need is around protecting the identity of the company that provides you with the information. This request is easy to meet because folks familiar with benchmarking know that the name on the company building is not what is important to know; rather, the steps in the process are the diamonds in the mine. So, any final report can provide information on companies A, B, and C, and it will be just as valuable. The last rule of effective benchmarking is that if you ask someone to participate in your study, you need to be comfortable that your company is also open to involvement in any benchmarking efforts that the respondent firms have under way or plan to launch in the future. Benchmarking is a two-way street.

Look Ahead

After the benchmarking effort has been completed, you are ready to begin the third phase of the process, namely, looking ahead. There are three general ways that this phase has been approached, and the path selected can make the difference between a disaster, a reasonable result, and an excellent conclusion to the project.

The first path that can be chosen is to try to exactly copy the process that someone else has been effectively using. For example, let's say you were interested in improving your team-based compensation approach for the sales force. In your research you repeatedly found references to IBM's approach to this issue. So, you contacted them and they were kind enough to give you detailed information on how they do it. Then, you took their precise approach and tried to introduce it wholesale into your organization. What will be the result? Most likely you will have a disaster of monumental proportions on your hands. The reason that the IBM process will blow up in your face is that if it worked so well for them, it must have matched their culture perfectly. The problem is that no one has a culture quite like IBM's. You cannot export IBM's process directly into any other firm and expect to see the same results.

The second general approach to looking ahead is to take someone else's process and try to adapt it to your own culture. This approach will lead to much better results than the copycat approach, but beware you will still not experience the same level of results that the benchmark firm has enjoyed.

The third path is to use your benchmarking information to identify the core performance concepts that allow a variety of firms to be successful in completing a process. Then, working with these concepts, find innovative ways to make them also work within the unique culture of your own firm. This is the surest path to success. For instance, if you are interested in improving your methods for inventory control, your research would undoubtedly lead you to L.L. Bean. The folks at L.L. Bean are justifiably well known for their expertise in this area. The reason for their success, however, can be traced to one core idea. That idea is that while there are many ways to handle inventory, such as stocking by size, color, manufacturer, and so on, there is clearly one best organizing concept, and that is frequency of turns. In other words, products should be allocated space in the warehouse based on their relative demand. The highest-turning items should be placed closest to receiving and shipping areas, followed by moderately turning items a little farther away, and so on. Once you know this concept, it can be easily utilized to respond to any firm's unique inventory control needs.

Take Action

This leads us to the fourth phase of the process improvement process, that is, to take action. Unless clear and well-informed steps are taken to implement the new changes correctly, nothing will come of the effort. These steps include surveying the members of the units impacted by the potential process changes to understand both their readiness for change and what must be done to prepare the group to adopt the changes. It also means that ways to measure process improvement have been put into place to indicate how much improvement has been realized from the effort. Likewise, one must ensure that feedback mechanisms have been established to provide ways for individuals doing the work to make additional suggestions for further improvements to the process. Finally, means need to be discussed and implemented for recognizing and rewarding efforts aimed at making the new process work as effectively and efficiently as possible.

IMPLEMENTING TEAM RECOMMENDATIONS

The last major issue that needs to be addressed in organizing a process improvement program is to decide who will implement the recommendations. Again, here we find that several approaches have been successfully used, and they likewise typically reflect cultural preferences within firms. One approach is to have the process improvement team responsible for implementing the recommendations. The rationale for this approach is that the requirement to implement the changes will bring about greater commitment on the part of the PIT to develop the best solution possible. Another approach is to have the process improvement team hand off a detailed implementation plan to the process users. This is clearly a variation of the staff-and-line model, where the staff does the analytical work and the line makes the changes happen in real time. The third approach is to have some select members of the process improvement team work with the process owners to work out the details of the implementation plan. This hybrid approach attempts to capture the best of the two other models. In all cases, however, the handoff protocol should be well known by all in advance of the actual event.

A CLOSER LOOK: TORRINGTON SUPPLY COMPANY

Torrington Supply Company is a third-generation, family-owned distributor of plumbing, heating equipment, pipe, values, and fittings. Since its founding in 1917, this family business has grown to become one of the largest and most profitable independent distributors of its product lines in Connecticut. Yet, along the way, the firm's road to success has not been without its challenges.

Indeed, as recently as 1990, the future of the firm looked very different. In that year, the leadership of the firm was passed to the third generation of the family, as Joel Becker became the new chairman and CEO, and his brother-in-law Fred Stein became the new president. It was also the first year in the company's 73-year history that the firm lost money.

As it took control of the firm, the new management knew that it faced a number of serious sales and operating issues. First, the regional economy had taken a tailspin over the previous 12 months and was deep in recession. This downturn contributed to a decline in sales. Second, the company had recently moved from a smaller, older, multistoried facility to a large, modern distribution center, but its operating model and cost structure were designed for the older facility. To make matters worse, the company had to take on new debt.

It was not until early 1992, when Joel attended an American Supply Association meeting in Atlanta, however, that the full nature of the firm's challenges and some possible solutions became more evident. At a session focusing on the findings of an Arthur Andersen/National Association of Wholesalers study about the dramatic changes affecting the wholesale-distribution industry, he learned that the traditional distributor's role would be changing rapidly in the future. Specifically, the old role of primarily providing credit, sales and marketing, technical, and delivery services would disappear. In its place, the successful distributor of the future would need to become an efficient, highly automated fulfillment house. In doing so, it was predicted that operating costs would drop to less than half of the then-current industry averages. At the same time, the customer of the future would require immediate delivery, error-free order processing, and a lower price. Therefore, wholesale distributors would have to improve efficiency as well as eliminate mistakes and the associated rework by implementing new technologies in order to compete in the future. Only those companies able to incorporate new systems and procedures to eliminate waste would survive.

The message was simple and clear. Almost immediately the company began to make changes. First, it implemented a simple computerized delivery tracking system and began to experiment with hand-held batch process scanners to validate picking accuracy. Both systems reduced mistakes, but they were cumbersome and added direct payroll costs.

Meanwhile, the search for a material handling or warehouse management software package continued because the senior management team knew that was where the majority of its operating costs were coming from. Eventually, early in 1995, the company felt that it had discovered a possible answer in a new software developed by Eclipse, Inc., which was the first fully integrated enterprise software system with a working material handling module.

The first phase of the new software implementation, which included the sales, purchasing, and financial modules, training, and new hardware, cost about $250,000 and required six months of intensive file maintenance work to prepare for the conversion. It also came at a time when the Connecticut economy was still in deep recession, and the company's reserves were needed to finance inventory and poor operating profits. The timing could not have been worse, but it was a move that the company's leaders felt they had to take in order to survive.

The company went live with the new software in September 1995. Two months later, the company began installing the warehouse management equipment and software module. This required the purchase and installation of scanning equipment, printers, a new software network and network wiring, and a host of other unforeseen items that almost doubled the initially budgeted costs. The initial budget called for 6 hand-held radio frequency bar-code scanners at $4,500 each. It quickly became apparent that sharing scanners was unrealistic and that everyone who touched material during the day needed a scanner, so 6 went to 19, which soon became 23.

Purchasing the new equipment was the easy part. To get ready for the next step in the conversion process required an intensive manual effort over several months to get the warehouse ready to receive bar-coded shipments.

In March 1996 the company began scanning all of its incoming shipments. This was a time-consuming and expensive process. When receiving material for the first time on the new system, the manufacturer's bar codes had to be entered into the company's computer system. This required scanning the incoming product and identifying in the computer the product that was scanned prior to actually receiving the product. At the time, only half the incoming material had manufacturer's bar codes. In these cases, bar code numbers had to be assigned, and bar code labels had to be printed, put on each box, and then scanned into the company's computer prior to receiving. This was a critical process because identification mistakes made here became outbound shipping errors later.

In June 1996, the outbound picking system was turned on. Initially, hardware problems were encountered that masked more significant problems related to how the work was being performed. The old mistakes were eliminated, but new, more complicated problems replaced them, and order-picking time skyrocketed. What took one minute in the old system now took 2 and 3 times as long. Service levels became unacceptable, and costs skyrocketed. It quickly became apparent that the way that the new system routed the picking process would not work for the company.

Responding to this latest challenge, a process improvement team consisting of managers, warehouse personnel, and Eclipse software engineers held a series of conference calls to redesign the system to meet the requirements of the pickers and incorporate the efficiencies and tracking capabilities of the new software. This process improvement effort took almost two months and was expanded to include representatives from sales, purchasing, and finance. Over the next year, the resulting changes recommended by the process team and implemented by the company impacted almost all of the firm's core activities.

Fortunately, the results were immediate and resounding. The company estimates that the direct payroll savings in the first year alone were around $255,000. The company also doubled its net operating profit in each of the following 3 years. In addition, based on pre- and postimplementation survey results, customer and employee satisfaction also increased.

Most importantly, a culture developed in the organization of looking for ways to automate and standardize processes wherever possible. Over the next year, every process that was repetitive and followed predictable patterns became a target for being automated and controlled by the computer. Everyone in the company realized that if he or she could eliminate time spent on managing repetitive company functions, they could devote more quality time to customers.

Today, all receiving, picking, cycle counting, shipping and routing, invoicing, purchasing, outside sales tracking, and billing are tracked and directed for maximum efficiency by the computer. Routine, clerical, non-value-added functions, such as bill reconciliation and invoice filing, were eliminated when the company eliminated paper from its billing process. Additionally, the company eliminated paper from its purchasing process using direct faxing, Electronic Data Interfacing (EDI), and other non-people processes for all functions possible. The automated delivery routing system improved the company's shipping efficiency by 25% while simultaneously eliminating the need for a shipping dispatcher and providing the sales department with immediate, accurate, and dependable shipping information. Delivery personnel now use a PalmPilot for routing and delivery signature-capture.

By early 1997, the company realized that it could now build its growth strategy around its core operating competences. Accordingly, an active hub-and-spoke branching strategy was initiated that has led to the opening of five branches over the last three years. These branches provide local customer contact and intimacy, while the efficient procurement and order fulfillment systems work behind the scenes to give each branch the customer services of much larger companies. Thus, in an industry with average sales per employee of $250-300 thousand, Torrington's branches operate at $500-750 thousand sales per employee.

In summary, by taking a long-term view towards continuously improving the most essential parts of their business, Torrington Supply Company has shown how it is possible to reap the benefits of a concerted quality effort. Mounting revenues, higher levels of profitability as well as increasing external and internal customer satisfaction attest to the value of this approach. Opening one door has led into another room of opportunity. Indeed, today they are exploring how to use the information being captured in their system to build better customer profiles for the future (Becker, 1999). What additional opportunities will present themselves, no one knows. What is clear is that this company's "paperless warehouse" will permit the firm to be a formidable competitor in the future.

REFERENCES

Becker, J. 1999. Personal interview. December 7, Waterbury, CT.

Bounds, G. M. 1996. *Cases in quality.* Chicago: Irwin.

Camp, R. C. 1995. *Business process benchmarking: Finding and implementing best practices.* Milwaukee, WI: ASQC Press.

Camp, R. C. 1989. *Benchmarking: The search for industry best practices that lead to superior performance.* Milwaukee, WI: Quality Press.

Fairfield-Sonn, J.W. 1999. Influence of context on process improvement teams: Leadership from a distance. *Journal of Business and Economic Studies,* 5 (2): 61–80.

Garvin, D. A. 1995. Leveraging processes for strategic advantage: A roundtable with Xerox's Allaire, USAA's Herres, SmithKline Beecham's Leschly, and Pepsi's Weatherup. *Harvard Business Review,* 73 (5): 76–90.

Heifetz, R. A. 1994. *Leadership without easy answers.* Cambridge: Harvard University Press.

Juran, J. M. 1988. *Juran on planning for quality.* New York: Free Press.

Main, J. 1992. How to steal the best secrets around. *Fortune,* October 19: 102–106.

Pine, J. B., II, & Gilmore, J. H. 1998. Welcome to the experience economy. *Harvard Business Review,* 76 (4): 97–105.

Port, O., & Smith, G. 1992. Beg, borrow, and benchmark. *Business Week,* November 30: 74–75.

Porter, M. E. 1996. What is strategy? *Harvard Business Review,* 74 (6): 61-78.

Scholtes, P. R., Joiner, B. L. & Streibel, B. J. 1996. *The team handbook*. 2nd ed. Madison, WI: Joiner Associates.

Taguchi, G., & Clausing, D. 1990. Robust quality. *Harvard Business Review*, 68 (1): 65–75.

Zack, M. H., & McKenney, J. L. 1996. Social context and interaction in ongoing computer-supported management groups. *Organization Science*, 6 (4): 394–422.

Chapter 7

Developing People

Effective management is the productive use of strengths.

—Peter Drucker, 1999

Earlier we talked about the importance of building a solid foundation for a quality effort. That effort was likened to building a house. However, we all know that a house is not a home. A house is just a structure. A home is a place where individuals can go to find a sense of community and belonging as well as to do good work. Many organizations have historically been satisfied merely to provide a house where work could be done. Quality organizations, on the other hand, know that it is equally important to create a work environment where individuals can also grow personally and professionally. The focus of this chapter is on exploring how to make this larger view of the workplace a reality.

INTERNAL AND EXTERNAL NEEDS

At a minimum, to create an enriched and rewarding work-place environment requires a desire on the part of employers to discover and appreciate employee needs (Friedman, Christensen, and DeGroot 1998). Specifically, it has been recognized for some time that people are motivated, in varying degrees, by the need to fulfill two types of needs at work. One set of needs is "internal," and the other is "external" (Herzberg, Mausner, and Synderman, 1959).

More precisely, internal needs are based on meeting the unique desires that individuals have around such *intangible* issues as being able to do meaningful work; being given sufficient autonomy to do a job; and being granted the authority to make decisions in areas where they have accountability for results. External needs, on the other hand, are addressed by providing *tangible* rewards and recognition in the form of base salaries, bonus plans, stock options, and various employee recognition programs (e.g., employee of the month). So, while the content and relative importance of these drives vary across individuals as well as within individuals over time (Covey, 1989), both are important for employers to consider because they impact employees' performance by either increasing or decreasing employees' levels of satisfaction and commitment to the firm.

What does an organization get in return for meeting these needs? Internal motivators have been shown to strongly influence how hard and passionately an individual will work on any given task. Indeed, when internal motivation is high, individuals will often willingly exceed minimum performance expectations. On the other hand, external motivators have been shown to be more useful in keeping individuals working for an organization.

Given that these two types of motivators can be instrumental in fostering desirable, albeit rather different, behaviors, it is clearly in the best interest of firms desiring to promote a quality culture to provide both stimulating work assignments as well as fair and consistent rewards and recognition (Lawler, Mohrman, and Ledford 1992). This is because employees in quality organizations must be willing to go beyond just meeting minimum performance requirements, and as they grow personally and professionally, their potential to contribute to the organization increases over time (Drucker, 1999). In this chapter, the internal side of the motivation equation is examined. In the next chapter, the external side is explored to reveal its impact on performance.

MOTIVATING WORK

In addition to knowing employees' needs, to create an enriched and motivating work environment, it is also necessary for employers to proactively seek ways to give employees work assignments that they experience as motivating. Here, a recognition of the importance of two interrelated characteristics of work assignments can be helpful in understanding their potential to motivate employees to do their best work. First, to what degree are assignments viewed by employees as stimulating and challenging? Second, how will the employee be asked to complete the assignment?

For example, two financial analysts may like to work on accounting problems. However, one of these analysts might prefer to set up the systems to address accounting issues, while the other gains greater pleasure from actually running the numbers. In addition, the first analyst might like to work independently to reach a final proposed solution, while the other analyst likes to have constant feedback on how well she is doing. Both of these employees can be great assets to any organization, but their performance will be a function of how well their assignments "fit" their personal work preferences.

This illustration sheds some light on a pervasive management concern, namely, why attempts to motivate employees often lead to mixed results. That is, why do some employees work harder in response to various motivational techniques such as threats or encouragement, yet other employees hardly change at all, and, in the worst case, performance actually continues to decline despite the manager's best efforts to motivate the individual?

The reason for the mixed results can often be found in a common faulty assumption. Specifically, many managers and supervisors believe that "work is work." You get paid to work, so whatever assignment I give you should be done with equal vigor. While this assumption seems reasonable, it flies in the face of much that we know about how individuals' skills and interests develop over time.

More precisely, over the last several decades a substantial body of research has accumulated that indicates that individuals have preferences for different types of work, which begin to surface very early in life (Levinson, 1989). For example, successful entrepreneurs have often begun their first new venture(s) in their teenage years, future scientists begin experimenting with novel ways to use existing technology in elementary school, and so on. These differences in interests and skills, moreover, become more pronounced over time. Eventually, a pattern emerges that can be useful in predicting how successful an individual will be in a variety of positions. Thus, when managers offer employees assignments that tap into their natural internal motivation patterns, good things happen. Asking employees to do things that they are not themselves motivated to do, on the other hand, is an invitation to frustration and disappointment for both parties (Miller and Mattson, 1989).

A General Diagnostic Model

To make this point clear, consider the following example based on the use of a simple, yet powerful, diagnostic model. To understand why work assignments are more or less motivating to different individuals, you can divide work along two dimensions. One dimension is the degree to which an individual is good or bad at a task. The other dimension is the degree to which an individual likes or dislikes the task (Figure 7.1).

In this illustration, we can see that the individual likes to do planning and is good at it. In other words, she is good at planning, likes to do planning, and, all things being equal, would prefer to be involved in planning efforts. Indeed, if she could work almost exclusively in this area, her internal motivation would be at a peak level, and not only she but the organization as a whole would benefit from this appropriate matching of interests, skills, and job requirements.

Figure 7.1
Influence of Work Assignments on Motivation

Nature of Work

	Good at	Bad at
Like	Planning	Making presentations
Dislike	Administration	Entertaining clients

At the same time, we can see that while she is good at administration, she really does not like to do it. If no one in the organization knows how much she dislikes administration, her boss(es) might draw the incorrect conclusion that she would welcome more administrative responsibilities. In fact, this type of assignment is very frustrating for her, and if management is not open to hearing this, the employee may be asked to spend more, not less, time on this type of activity. The result, over the long term, is that she would probably suffer burnout and might even start looking for work somewhere else. In that case, the employee and the employer would lose.

Moreover, from this diagnosis we can see that while she likes to make presentations, she is bad at them. Once this fact is known, she and management are empowered to make more effective joint career-planning decisions. One path to follow would be to have another employee present the results of her planning efforts and thus save her from a potentially damaging career experience. The other path would be to look at making presentations as an opportunity for personal and professional development. In other words, with appropriate coaching and counseling, she might be able to develop this skill to the point where it could become another professional asset for her in her career progression.

Finally, we can see that she does not like to entertain clients, and she is bad at it. This is a work assignment that needs to be avoided, if at all possible, because she not only lacks skills in this area but is also not motivated to engage in this activity. Asking her to get involved in this type of assignment would hurt the organization and the employee.

In summary, in this illustration, we find an individual who is an excellent planner. On the other hand, this individual would not be very good at presenting the results of the plan to others or in administering the plan after it has been drafted. Moreover, she would definitely not be good at selling the plan to outsiders. Accordingly, in a perfect world her work would be limited to internal planning.

In reality, we all know that this cannot happen. Everyone has some elements of his or her job that he or she doesn't like. The key to successfully motivating employees, therefore, is to proactively try to maximize the amount of time that they spend doing the kind of work that they find rewarding and minimize their time spent on unrewarding activities.

Gaining Deeper Insights

While the preceding diagnostic tool can lead to some useful, general insights, some employers want a deeper analysis and a more systematic way to reveal the motivators that lie deep within each and every person. If this is your desire, there are many methods available to fulfill this need. Foremost among these approaches is a methodology pioneered by People Management, Inc., called a System for Identifying Motivated Abilities (SIMA) (Miller and Mattson, 1989).

The SIMA methodology is based on asking people to recall a number of achievements that they enjoyed doing and believe were done well. In analyzing these enjoyable achievement experiences, a consistent, recurring pattern called a Motivated Abilities Pattern, MAP®, emerges. This pattern helps to answer a number of important questions about job fit. Specifically, what abilities a person is motivated to use (e.g., persuasion), the subject matter that he or she likes to work on (e.g., people issues), circumstances within which a person is motivated to work (e.g., novel situations), the type of relationship that an individual is motivated to establish (e.g., team member), and the results that he or she is motivated to accomplish (e.g., build things) become apparent.

Knowledge of these motivating factors can, in turn, provide invaluable guidance to individuals and employers about the kind of work assignments that any specific individual will find rewarding and thus where that person can make the greatest contribution to an organization.

GETTING FEEDBACK

The third key element in creating an enriched and rewarding work environment is to provide employees with rich, accurate, and ongoing feedback on how well they are doing with their assignments. In other words, while it is necessary for employees to receive challenging assignments matched to their deeper internal needs to be fully engaged at work, doing so will still not guarantee that employees can grow in their job. Specifically, in the absence of rich feedback employees cannot attain their full potential because they are not given sufficient information to learn what actions led to more or less effective performance, perceived or real (Argyris, 1998; Spreitzer, 1995).

Historically, this has been an area where traditional, hierarchical organizations have been particularly weak. In contrast, continuous improvement organizations have viewed the feedback process as a distinctive opportunity for employee development, and thus more emphasis has been placed on it.

Multirater Feedback

The reason for divergent views on the benefits of providing feedback to employees can be found deep in the structure and worldviews that dominate these two models of how to organize and run a firm. Specifically, in traditional organizations, the performance appraisal process has often been more narrowly defined as a way for a boss and subordinates to set, monitor, and evaluate progress toward organizational goals. So, when the boss is pleased with the subordinate, for any number of reasons, good evaluations follow. At the same time, the "boss" has considerable license to also give bad evaluations to employees who do not meet any of his or her personal expectations.

In contrast, in a process-oriented workplace it is understood that while a subordinate works for a boss, and bosses' opinions are important, employee effectiveness is also a function of how well he or she meets the needs of customers, peers, suppliers, and so on. Accordingly, the opinions of all of these constituents need to be considered in creating a more rounded view of the overall contribution that is being made by the employee.

Given this perspective, it does not make much sense in a customer-focused, continuous improvement work environment to argue that an individual's contribution should be determined primarily or solely by his or her official boss, particularly since managers and supervisors are now so often stretched that they cannot see the work of their so-called direct reports. Instead, a better approach is to have multiple raters (i.e., peers, customers, etc.) collectively involved in the evaluation.

Ongoing Feedback

In a traditional organization, the performance appraisal often is an annual event. That is, at the end of the year the boss and the subordinate sit down to review the employee's overall performance for the year. This approach often leads to unsatisfactory discussions and conclusions for three basic reasons. One reason is that too much information must be condensed into a single session. The second reason is that the employee may find out too late in the year that for a variety of reasons, his or her performance was being viewed as unsatisfactory. Naturally, the frustration for the employee comes from the fact that it is now too late to do anything about it. Third, in any disagreement, the boss will be "right" based on organizational authority, and the employee is "wrong" because he or she lacks the formal power to challenge the judgment.

The alternative to this approach that is being actively pursued in continuous improvement organizations is to provide ongoing coaching as a means to enhance employee commitment to the firm (Kinlaw, 1989). Specifically, four distinctive types of coaching have been shown to enhance employee development efforts in a variety of situations. First, where an employee needs to vent strong feelings, a counseling approach can be helpful. Second, if an employee needs to develop greater sensitivity to the organization's culture and gain greater commitment to the organization's goals and values, mentoring is useful. Third, when an individual's technical competence needs to be enhanced, tutoring is appropriate. Finally, when concerns arise around performance expectations, then a confronting approach is in order.

INVOLVEMENT IN QUALITY IMPROVEMENT

One of the common challenges that must be faced in introducing a continuous improvement program is that old ways of thinking about individuals' roles in an organization need to change. For example, in a traditional command-and-control work environment individuals learn that doing your job in the manner prescribed by management is the safest and most likely to be rewarded approach to work. In contrast, in a continuous improvement environment individuals need to take the initiative in improving their work processes and the work processes of others.

It is often assumed, therefore, that the key to employee involvement in a continuous improvement effort lies primarily in changing individuals' attitudes about the importance of doing a good job. There is some obvious truth in this belief. However, this truth is only partial. A better statement of reality is that while attitude change is a necessary condition for effective participation in a continuous improvement effort, it is not sufficient (Fishbein and Ajzen, 1975). Specifically, to make a real contribution, individuals must also want to get involved in this type of activity, receive ongoing coaching on how to more effectively use quality improvement tools and techniques, and be rewarded for their efforts (Cole, Bacdayan, and White, 1993).

Desire to Participate

In other words, involvement in process improvement can be a satisfying task for some individuals, but it is not for everyone. Specifically, individuals who like this direction will feel assured that there is a place for them in the long-term plans of the firm. At the same time, other employees will recognize that they really do not want to be part of this kind of organization. In this case, they can proactively start to search for another organization to work for. Individuals who see only a partial job fit, meanwhile, can try to find ways to redefine their responsibilities. Thus, over the long term everyone wins.

This is true for executives, middle managers, front-line supervisors, and rank-and-file employees. When an organization decides to become process-oriented, it may mean that many formerly "good" employees will decide to leave the firm or be asked to leave because they do not embrace this new philosophy of management. Clearly, this happened at both SmithKline Beecham and Pepsi, where almost all the senior management team was replaced after the decision was made to become a process-oriented firm (Garvin, 1995).

Coaching on How to Contribute

Likewise, the "right" kind of training and development must be offered, or no improvement will be seen. For example, the senior management of a major chemical company became very frustrated after the firm had devoted two years and several million dollars to a training and development effort aimed at improving attitudes toward quality, which led to little improvement. Naturally, the top officials of the firm initially thought that the root cause of the failure could be attributed to a weakness in the training effort. Accordingly, they were preparing to revise the program and try again.

Before moving forward with this plan, however, they decided to study the situation more carefully. The study (Procopio and Fairfield-Sonn, 1996) yielded some surprising results. Specifically, they discovered that most of the employees already believed in the fundamental principles and value of quality improvement. What they lacked was sufficient knowledge of the basic tools and techniques to make it happen. In other words, while the employees wanted to enhance their work processes, they were not receiving sufficient ongoing coaching to learn how to use the tools and techniques more effectively on their projects. Based on this analysis, the firm changed the focus of its training effort to concentrate on providing skill-based, on-the-job training. Within two months of the launch of the new program noticeable improvements in quality were being realized by the company in many of its operations.

Being Rewarded for Participation

Finally, one of the most important tasks related to establishing high levels of internal motivation is to clearly link individual development plans to the firm's strategic objectives. This simple act of clarifying where individuals need to focus can be extremely helpful in enhancing the motivation of all employees. To achieve this new state of physical and mental engagement, however, individuals need to be empowered by their superiors to take action. Here, we encounter a major challenge in transforming an organization's culture. Namely, while managers and employees may publicly say that they want to foster empowerment, in reality, neither party may actually want it (Argyris, 1998). Only true efforts will succeed.

Some Ways to Support the Effort

There are many ways for employers to demonstrate their concern about, and commitment to, the personal and professional development of their employees, as illustrated by the efforts at several Baldrige Award-winning firms. For example, at Sunny Fresh Foods, a food-processing company, there is a general concern about employees' potentially suffering from repetitive stress injuries. To address this concern, the firm has instituted a policy that every employee must rotate to a new workstation every 20 minutes. Internal studies reveal that this step has not only reduced the number of injuries reported but also reduced boredom and increased the quality of the work produced. At Solectron, all employees receive a minimum number of hours of training each year. In 1995 this minimum was 160 hours, which is extremely high compared to any industry average. This training is broad in scope. It includes training in the use of quality tools, computer systems, cross-functional education, and even English as a second language. Meanwhile, at Solar Turbines in the early 1990s its entire approach to employee management was transformed from administering salaries and benefits to becoming a powerful force for change. As part of this change it abandoned its traditional approach to boosting productivity by adding more material, capital, and labor. In their place, they set their sights on finding ways to increase productivity by fostering initiative and capabilities within a self-directed workforce. In this "pro-employee" approach to work system teaming, the company does not differentiate between union and nonunion workers. Instead, developing people, rather than overseeing tasks, has become the primary job of managers and supervisors.

A CLOSER LOOK: GENERAL ELECTRIC

During the last decade the fantastic growth of revenues and profits at General Electric (GE) under the leadership of Jack Welch has been the source of awe, inspiration, and concern, depending on the perspective of the observer. While Welch gets much of the credit for this enviable record, he and others within the firm are quick to explain that these results would never have been achieved without a systematic method for identifying and grooming talent within the firm. That method, the GE method, has been refined over the last several decades to a high art form at a lovely, isolated campus called Crotonville in Ossining, New York. As every headhunter in the country knows, it works.

Crotonville launched its first 13-week advanced management program in 1956. Since that time it has grown in stature as a grooming and proving ground for future managers at GE. Starting with its birth, it has also served as a pulpit for succeeding generations of GE presidents to convey their message of the day. No one, however, has used it as effectively as Jack Welch, who early on saw its potential as a vehicle for changing the culture of GE through the development of a new breed of leader (Tichy, 1989).

More precisely, when Welch became CEO of GE in 1981, he recognized the enormous potential of the firm but also that the bureaucratic culture of the company would need to be changed to release the potential pent up in the organization. To attack this inherited culture head-on, he likewise knew he would need a place to begin challenging the old values and start shaping the values for the future.

To turn this vision into a reality, Welch recruited James Baughman from Harvard Business School and charged him with reshaping the curriculum focus, teaching methods, and the faculty composition at Crotonville (Tichy, 1989). Over the next several years a major transformation began that continues today. In essence, what Baughman started was a movement away from teaching primarily hard (e.g., finance, manufacturing) cognitive skills to a combination of hard and soft (e.g., recruiting, teamwork) leadership skills. Moreover, the target audience was expanded from primarily working with the firm's executives to all levels of management. At the same time, the preferred method of instruction changed from a classroom format to a more GE problem-based workshop format structured around the principles of action learning (Marquardt, 1999). This method emphasizes learning by wrestling with real-life problems and then having an opportunity to reflect both on what was learned and how it was learned. Finally, to add more punch to the workshops, increasingly, GE executives were recruited to run the workshop sessions.

While all of these programs are highly effective, the most distinctive is the series offered for executives. The first course in this series is called the Management Development Course (MDC). This three-week residential course is for "younger," high-potential executives. It is structured like a mini-M.B.A. with every GE division being allotted slots for this course based on the revenue of the unit. Every year six to seven groups, consisting of approximately 65 cross-functional participants each, attend the program. This course is taught by a combination of GE leaders and academics from preeminent undergraduate and graduate schools.

The objective of this course is multifaceted. One primary goal is simply to enhance general management skills. Another major goal is to reinforce the key performance measurements used to run GE. But MDC, like all leadership training programs at GE, is strategically viewed as much more than a primer on business fundamentals. In many cases, class members are interacting with leadership peers from outside their business for the first time in their careers. So, for these three weeks, they are relieved of their regular responsibilities and encouraged to share common operational challenges and successes with colleagues from the vast array of GE businesses. The result is boundaryless learning as peers from unrelated markets explore their experiences and solutions to common problems. From this experience, fresh perspectives are taken back to participants' business units and aggressively shared.

The second course in this series is called the Business Management Course (BMC). This three-week course focuses on nurturing strategic leadership skills and exposing the participants to key global initiatives within the company. Participants in this course are nominated by each division's leadership during the annual staffing review and approved for attendance by the president of the business unit. Therefore, BMC attendees are typically high-potential functional leaders who have demonstrated their ability to deliver outstanding results within current and previous assignments. Moreover, class members are likely to be slated for a more responsible position within the following year.

Usually, the BMC is held off-campus at a global location with attractive current or future GE market opportunities. The first week of the course is spent grounding the class on fundamental economic, social, political, and commercial issues associated with the countries or region sponsoring the BMC. In the second week, participants are presented with a real business challenge facing a GE unit in the region. For example, recently, one GE business was looking to develop a market entry strategy for a region of the world where it had virtually no market presence. A class team was formed, comprising exclusively of participants who did not work in the sponsoring business, to develop a proposal for how the sponsoring GE business could capture 30% market share within two years.

After receiving their assignments, the teams work effectively as management consulting organizations. Teams are given a week to explore the issues and craft an actionable business plan. During this time, team members meet with a cross-section of people who live with, or can influence, the issues under consideration. They gather opinions from local business leaders, customers, academics, civic leaders, and key suppliers. In light of this information, the teams develop a proposal, refine their recommendations, test ideas, and create a formal presentation. The capstone of the BMC is a return to Crotonville and a spirited delivery of the findings and recommendations to CEO Jack Welch and the leaders of each of the GE businesses. The learning is intense, and the feedback is quite informative.

The third course in the series is called the Executive Development Course (EDC). This class is reserved for individuals who have been identified as possessing the potential to become officers within the company during the next year or two. Welch personally approves all these participants. The format here is much like that of the BMC, except that the target issues (e.g., developing new sourcing strategies, how to enter e-commerce alliances) are much broader and more strategic in their scope.

If these courses sound challenging, they are, but from GE's experience they are also the best way to broaden seasoned executives, and, as noted earlier, they work.

In summary, the importance of helping employees to recognize their natural strengths, weaknesses, and motivational drives, such that they can develop personally and professionally at work, is becoming ever more critical to the long-term success of organizations. The reason for this shift is easy to understand.

Success in today's jobs requires that employees put their heart and mind into work. Just having a body present to complete assignments for eight hours a day is insufficient. To develop higher levels of commitment from an employee, however, an organization must commit to working closely with each individual to help him or her to craft and pursue a personal development plan that meets his or her needs today and for the future and a workplace environment where contribution to the pursuit of quality is respected and rewarded.

REFERENCES

Argyris, C. 1998. Empowerment: The emperor's new clothes. *Harvard Business Review*, 76 (3): 98–105.

Cole, R. E., Bacdayan, P. & White, B. J. 1993. Quality, participation, and competitiveness. *California Management Review*, 35 (3): 68–81.

Covey, S. R. 1989. *The 7 habits of highly effective people*. New York: Simon & Schuster.

Drucker, P. F. 1999. Managing oneself. *Harvard Business Review*, 77 (2): 65–74.

Fishbein, M., & Ajzen, I. 1975. *Beliefs, attitude, intention, and behavior: An introduction to theory and research*. Reading, MA: Addison-Wesley.

Friedman, S. D., Christensen, P. & DeGroot, J. 1998. Work and life: The end of the zero-sum game. *Harvard Business Review*, 76 (6): 119–129.

Garvin, D. A. 1995. Leveraging processes for strategic advantage: A roundtable with Xerox's Allaire, USAA's Herres, SmithKline Beecham's Leschly, and Pepsi's Weatherup. *Harvard Business Review*, 73 (5): 76–90.

Herzberg, F., Mausner, B. & Synderman, B. 1959. *The motivation to work*. New York: John Wiley & Sons.

Kinlaw, D. C. 1989. *Coaching for commitment: Managerial strategies for obtaining superior performance*. San Diego: Pfeiffer.

Lawler, E. E., III, Mohrman, S. A. & Ledford, G. A. Jr. 1992. *Employee involvement and total quality management: Practices and results in Fortune 1,000 companies*. San Francisco: Jossey-Bass.

Levinson, H. 1989. *Designing and managing your career*. Boston: Harvard Business School Press.

Marquardt, M. J. 1999. *Action learning in action: Transforming problems and people for world-class organizational learning.* Palo Alto, CA: Davies-Black.

Miller, A. F., Jr., & Mattson, R. T. 1989. *The truth about you.* Berkeley, CA: Ten Speed Press.

Procopio, A. J., & Fairfield-Sonn, J. W. 1996. Changing attitudes towards quality: An exploratory study. *Group & Organization Management,* 21 (2): 133–145.

Spreitzer, G. 1995. Psychological empowerment in the workplace: Dimensions, measurement, and validation. *Academy of Management Journal,* 38 (5): 1442–1465.

Tichy, N. 1989. GE's Crotonville: A staging ground for corporate revolution. *Academy of Management Executive,* 3 (2): 99–106.

Chapter 8

Recognizing and Rewarding Performance

Soldiers don't die for their country, they die for the chance to win a medal.

—Napoleon Bonaparte

A cultural transformation must begin as a grand vision, but it will never take hold in a firm until new attitudes and behaviors are appropriately recognized and rewarded. The transformation to a quality organization is no exception to this rule. To become a way of life within an organization, quality initiatives must be consciously nurtured and sustained through visible and equitable recognition and rewards. In the absence of these concrete and genuine signs of appreciation for contributions made to the achievement of key organizational quality goals, the quality effort is doomed to meet a slow and painful death.

YOU GET WHAT YOU PAY FOR

Over two decades ago, Steven Kerr (1975) wrote what has become a classic article on how to think about establishing an effective recognition and reward system. The title of his article, "On the Folly of Rewarding A, While Hoping for B," gives away the ending. His advice, readily grasped from the title, is that in the long run you get only what you pay for.

Why Recognition and Reward Systems Often Miss the Mark

This commonsense advice may sound simplistic. Yet, as we so often find, the problem with good commonsense advice is that there is too little common practice of it. This is certainly true of recognition and reward systems. Too often they miss their mark for one or more of the following frequently observed reasons.

One classic problem noted by Kerr (1975) is the fascination with "objective" criteria. For example, he cites the case of an insurance company that was interested in performance but made all its raises conditional on good attendance (i.e., a clear, objective behavioral measure). What the firm got were bodies coming to work. How much work employees did once they arrived, however, made very little difference in determining their final pay raises. So, performance continued to be mediocre.

Another major problem with recognition and reward systems is their overemphasis on highly visible behaviors. For instance, despite their claims to care about teaching, most universities reward publications more generously than classroom performance. The reason for this is that it is easier to see an article or book than to see what a teacher does in the classroom to stimulate the thinking of students (Kerr, 1975). In the same vein, many organizations will more readily recognize and reward the timely completion of projects and reports than the efforts made by contributors to these efforts to be good team players in the production effort itself.

The third major cause of problems with recognition and reward systems is hypocrisy (Kerr, 1975); that is, management rewards activities (e.g., apple-polishing) that it publicly admonishes. It doesn't take employees too long to discover what is really going to be rewarded. Once employees make this discovery, that is what management will get.

Designing a System That Delivers

The real rub for employees, however, often comes only during the first formal evaluation when they realize, in the worst-case scenario, for the first time what goals they are actually being held accountable for attaining. In the remainder of this chapter, we explore some ways to overcome these problems by bringing a quality discipline to the design and development of reward and recognition systems.

At their heart, the recognition and reward systems within most firms consist of a series of processes that are more or less integrated to organizational goals, and this is the root cause of many of the problems that are encountered. Too often there is insufficient understanding by the system designers that all the recognition and reward processes need to be based on a common model and that all of the processes need to be linked together to lead to a consistent end result.

More precisely, to create an effective recognition and reward system, the first question that needs to be addressed is, What is the purpose of our system? Without a widely held agreement on this fundamental issue, it is unlikely that an effective system will ever be put in place.

There are three basic answers to this question, and each answer carries with it enormous implications for how the system will function. One answer is to design a system that will recognize and reward contributions made to the completion of a specific job. This "task-oriented" approach focuses primarily on what work needs to get done today. Working under this model, individuals are selected and assigned to jobs based on the degree to which they already have the necessary technical skills to immediately begin working on the tasks at hand. They will receive little or no additional training in these jobs because they already know how to do the work. Their recognition and rewards will, in all likelihood, come primarily from units of work produced (Figure 8.1).

Figure 8.1
Three Purposes of Recognition and Reward Systems

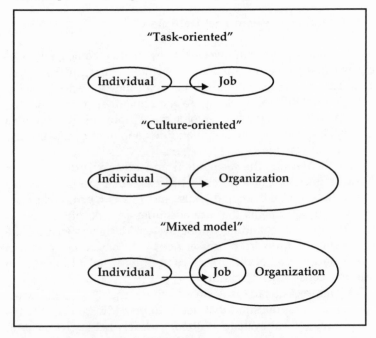

Another answer is to design a "culture-oriented" system. This model assumes that the congruence between an individual's values and the values of the firm will be the best predictor of long-term success. In other words, if the value fit is right, then an employee can be taught the technical aspects of most jobs. Thus, recognition and rewards under this approach will be contingent foremost upon making a contribution to the organization, writ large, and then in your area of technical specialization.

The third answer is to develop a "mixed model" system. Here, organizations are striving to reach a balance in emphasizing the importance of both technical skills and organizational fit. Working under this model, employees may or may not receive much additional training and development, depending on what assignments they are asked to take on over time. Likewise, recognition and rewards will vary as a function of what particular work that the employee is being asked to complete.

WHAT'S IN IT FOR ME?

At the end of the day, all employees want to feel that they have been recognized and rewarded for their efforts to grow the organization. These visible indicators can take many forms, such as base pay, bonuses, stock options, and various forms of recognition (Zemke and Schaaf, 1989). They also want to know what kind of recognition and rewards others have received for their contributions. In other words, are rewards being equitably distributed throughout the organization or are some individuals or groups receiving more favorable treatment than others (de Geus, 1997)?

The answers to these questions will go a long way toward explaining how deeply a quality orientation will be woven into the fabric of the organization. In quality organizations the recognition and reward system is usually based more on a "culture-oriented" than on a "task-oriented" or "mixed" model preferred by more traditional organizations. Therefore, you typically see several distinctive characteristics of the system at work in quality organizations that distinguish them from the system operating in more traditional organizations.

First, monetary awards are given for providing outstanding customer service, but these awards are more often aimed at recognizing efforts that lead to long-term payoffs for the organization rather than primarily short-term payoffs for the individual employee. For example, the Great-West Life Assurance Company pays a 50% premium to group health insurance brokers who hit customer retention targets. The organization's goal here is to reward brokers for taking special care of customers who will stay with the company for a long time as opposed to just shopping and moving for price (Reichheld and Sasser, 1990).

Second, monetary rewards are more often given for successful group efforts rather than purely individual efforts. For instance, at MBNA, a major financial organization, each department has identified one or two things that have the greatest impact on customer retention. Each day when a department hits 95% of its goal in these areas MBNA contributes money to a bonus pool to be shared by all the employees in the department (Reichheld and Sasser, 1990).

The most distinctive characteristic of these systems within quality organizations, however, is their emphasis on the extensive use of recognition to reinforce the drive toward improvement. The reason for this approach is threefold. First, quality improvement needs to be everyone's goal, so everyone must believe that it is possible to be readily recognized for making a contribution (Bandura, 1977). Second, everyone must be encouraged to think about what is good for the organization as much as what is good for himself or herself (Lawler, Mohrman, and Ledford, 1992). Third, the long-term success of a continuous improvement effort rests more on the participation of many individuals' generating new ideas that can lead to breakthroughs as they are refined, rather than perfect ideas springing full-blown from the head of one individual (Plenert and Hibino, 1997).

If you are looking for more specific ideas on how to structure an effective recognition system, consider what Hodgetts, Kuratko, and Hornsby (1999) discovered as they analyzed the approaches taken by many Baldrige Award-winning companies. In these companies five common features were frequently observed. First, recognition is always positive and linked to actions that have led to success. Second, recognition is given openly and often publicized throughout the organization. Third, the form of recognition is carefully tailored to meet the needs of different employees. Fourth, rewards are given shortly after they have been earned. Fifth, the relationship between the achievement and the reward is clearly understood by the employees in the organization.

PUTTING TEETH INTO THE PROGRAM

To produce great results, individual commitment and passion are needed as well as technical knowledge. We have known for a long time that there are many ways to foster higher levels of commitment and passion in an organization (Meyer, Paunonen, Gellatly, Goffin, and Jackson, 1989; Ogilvie, 1986; Mowday, Porter, and Steers, 1982) . For example, the Romans created a simple system to enhance the motivation of their aqueduct architects. Indeed, this system may help to explain why many of these magnificent structures are still standing thousands of years after they were constructed. When the support scaffolding was removed from the keystone, the architect was standing underneath it. If there was a quality problem with the construction effort, the feedback was immediate and dramatic and solved the problem from ever recurring—at least by the architect who designed that particular structure.

Establishing clear linkages between performance and rewards is also seen today in many leading organizations. For instance, when Jack Welch of General Electric announces that no one will become an executive in the company until he or she has successfully led at least one process improvement team, folks get the message.

To get executives, in particular, to buy into a process management approach is a challenging task. Yet, nothing of much consequence will happen until they do. For many of these individuals their careers have been built on achieving departmental and individual goals for which they have been amply rewarded. To change their behaviors, there must be an appropriate change in the structure of the recognition and reward system. One approach that has worked well in a number of companies is to key bonus systems off a combination of organizational, departmental, and individual results. In this way, the rewards for taking a larger view of what needs to be done to move the enterprise forward as well as to receive the highest levels of personal recognition and rewards are easy to understand (Garvin, 1995).

Once the management team sees the benefits from embracing a new way of managing, it is a relatively simple matter to cascade this practice down into the organization at the team (Meyer, 1994) and individual level (Kaplan and Norton, 1993, 1992).

A CLOSER LOOK: CONNECTICUT RENAISSANCE

The benefits to be derived from fostering a continuous improvement culture are not limited to Fortune 500 giants, nor are they solely aimed at improving products and services for external customers. Nonprofit organizations have also benefited from successfully applying the tools and techniques of continuous improvement to their own concerns, which include the personal and professional development of staff members.

One notable example of a nonprofit that has used continuous improvement as an effective means to simultaneously grow the organization and enrich the lives of its employees is Connecticut Renaissance. This organization, founded in 1967 to provide drug rehabilitation services, traces the launch of its formal continuous improvement journey to 1994. In that year, with revenues of around $2.5 million, it completed its first formal strategic planning effort. As a result of those deliberations, the board and the senior management team decided that the time had come to introduce a continuous improvement focus into their activities as a way to enhance their overall competitiveness going forward.

What is interesting to note about this agency is that by the time it decided to introduce a continuous improvement focus into the organization, it had already established a strong track record of quality assurance. Indeed, it had already won several quality assurance awards such as the first Connecticut Association for Residential Facilities (CARF) Annual Program Service Award in 1989 and the Connecticut State Department of Corrections Contractor of the Year award in 1993 from accrediting bodies and customers.

Anyone familiar with the qualitative differences between quality assurance and continuous improvement efforts, however, knows that these two approaches have both strong philosophical differences as well as very different operational demand characteristics. Specifically, quality assurance is based on pursuing conformity to process demands and rigorous documentation that procedures are being followed. In contrast, as discussed throughout the earlier chapters of this book, continuous improvement is driven by the desire to identify processes most in need of improvement, to devise ways to enhance the process, and then to drive the needed changes into the organization as efficiently and effectively as possible. Accordingly, the challenge for organizations like Connecticut Renaissance is to blend two valuable philosophies and operating styles together into a coherent and comprehensive approach that utilizes the best features of both. This is best done by making continuous improvement the basis for analyzing and improving all processes with quality assurance as an overlay. In other words, it must become clear to everyone that every process is open to improvement. At the same time, after a process has been enhanced, a quality assurance effort will be applied to the process to ensure that it is being followed. In this way, the gains from the continuous improvement effort are captured in the short term and locked in for the long term.

Connecticut Renaissance experienced many early successes through its continuous improvement program. For example, using this methodology, it enhanced its database management program to more effectively capture client outcomes in a more systematic fashion. It also created the first formalized recruiting effort for the agency. Another particularly innovative use of the methodology was in the area of new product design. Specifically, when asked to bid on a state-sponsored driving while intoxicated (DWI) program, the agency did its homework and discovered that other providers had not been very successful in running these programs. To decide whether or not it should bid on this program, it began by benchmarking the processes being used by other providers to run this program. Based on this information it analyzed the current processes being used by other providers; found ways to improve on the processes to the point where it felt confident in being able to be successful where others had failed; and then submitted an innovative grant proposal based on its new delivery approach. It won the program grant, outcomes from the program exceeded anything previously experienced by other providers, and it has gone on to develop and sell a software package to help other agencies deliver the same type of program.

In 1999 the agency completed its third formal strategic planning effort. A key focus of these discussions was how to introduce a balanced scorecard system into the organization's performance appraisal system as a means of communicating the firm's strategy to all employees as well as recognizing and rewarding efforts that supported the organization's strategic goals.

To turn this goal into a reality, Executive Director Pat McAuliffe (1999) once again turned to his quality council to address a key organizational concern. As he reflected upon the effort, however, he decided not only to add another element to an already comprehensive evaluation and reward system but, rather, to use the introduction of the balanced scorecard as an opportunity to create a more unified and integrated performance appraisal system that would also reflect the agency's culture of continuous quality improvement.

Accordingly, his charge to the quality council was to organize a process improvement team that would integrate the current annual performance evaluation, quarterly evaluations, and training and development planning efforts as well as the bonus plan into one unified and simplified system that was legally defensible and would meet the requirements of all the agency's accrediting bodies. At the same time, a way was also needed to integrate the balanced scorecard method into the system. In launching the team, Pat encouraged it to think boldly about ways to identify and implement system, process, and procedure improvements throughout the entire array of evaluation mechanisms.

As the team began its work, it quickly realized that while the agency had a comprehensive set of evaluation processes, collectively it was far from integrated, effective, or efficient. Rather, over the years, the organization, like so many other firms, had created a patchwork quilt of evaluation mechanisms based on different forms and formats that did not provide very good guidance or feedback to employees on their overall short-term performance, much less specific guidance on how they should develop for the future. Moreover, filling out all these forms was viewed by many supervisors and employees as a waste of their time.

More precisely, when the team looked at the annual performance appraisal form, it concluded that it was too long, unfocused, and subjective to provide a truly useful measure of performance. As for the quarterly review process, the team felt that: it was likewise not very focused or helpful; it was not matched to the performance categories on the annual appraisal form; and it was of questionable value because all employees in the agency had to complete the form regardless of how long they had been at the agency or how well they had performed in the past. The training plan, meanwhile, consisted of a three-page guide to possible training needs with sections available for comments by supervisors and employees. Through internal discussions among team members, however, the team also discovered that the form was not being used by everyone in the agency. Indeed, one five-year veteran on the team confessed that she had never even seen the form. Upon closer inspection the bonus plan was seen to contain some potentially useful features in that it contained a balance of performance measures; each of the performance categories had weights; and a common form was being used. On the other hand, the team members concluded that its overall value was limited in that it had no relationship to the other evaluation processes; performance categories were being interpreted in different ways; and no one knew if the form would be used until a few days before it was announced that a bonus would be available, and then all the staff had to scramble to quickly fill out the forms.

Working over a four-month period of time, the team was able to make substantial progress in improving the overall evaluation system. The analysis led to a single uniform form with the following desirable characteristics. The annual appraisal form was shortened in length and divided into the four balanced scorecard categories of financial, operational, customer satisfaction, and learning and innovation results. In addition, each employee's job description, which would change with any significant change in responsibilities, now appeared on the cover of the appraisal form.

Regarding the quarterly reviews, the team decided to use the same format for this evaluation as the one used for the annual performance appraisal. In this way, an employee could readily see how each quarterly evaluation led up to the final annual performance appraisal ratings. In addition, it was decided that quarterly reviews would be mandatory only for first-year employees. After that time, an employee, for whatever reason, could request that a quarterly review be completed, and it would be until she or he felt that it was no longer necessary. Likewise, a supervisor, for whatever reason, could decide that it would be beneficial for an employee to continue receiving quarterly evaluations, and this would occur until the supervisor felt that it was no longer necessary. These changes were beneficial in a number of ways. First, by following this new process the total time devoted to this task was estimated to decrease from 420 hours/year to 180 hour/year. Perhaps even more importantly, this new system generated a number of valuable qualitative benefits as well. Foremost among these benefits was an increase in motivation to complete the forms because only those individuals who could benefit from the process were involved in it. Second, less time was devoted to tracking down the forms because again only those individuals who knew they needed the feedback were completing them. Third, the reason for completing the forms was now obvious and meaningful to all parties involved in the process.

A new training and development system was also designed to be a complement to the other performance appraisal processes. Specifically, within two weeks of establishing performance goals for the upcoming year, each employee would now meet with his or her supervisor to discuss and identify his or her training and development needs for the coming year. Once these goals were agreed to, they become a part of the annual appraisal form to be tracked throughout the year.

Meanwhile, the bonus system was significantly simplified by merely having it keyed to the annual performance appraisal process. Since each employee's rating at the end of the year could be determined against a 100-point base system, it was easy to use these ratings to determine the relative ranking of each employee against all other employees, and this rating, in turn, could be used to calculate the level of bonus that an employee was entitled to receive.

Once the improved system was designed, however, there were still concerns that it would not be used properly. For example, how could the organization be sure that some supervisors were not inflating their evaluations or being overly harsh in their evaluations? Along the same lines, there was a concern that some supervisors might insist on quarterly evaluations for too long a period of time or that employees might not want to move beyond this frequent feedback system. To address these concerns, the agency went one step further to design a quality assurance measure on the back end of the system. Specifically, each year, shortly after the appraisals were completed, an audit team would review all the evaluations for patterns of ratings that might suggest further process improvements or training needs for the future.

In summary, this chapter focused on the importance of designing an appropriate and effective recognition and reward system, if you ever hope to make continuous improvement a way of life within a firm. While there are many ways to approach this critical task, discussed here was why the best way is to focus on creating a "culture-oriented" system that provides ample recognition and rewards for everyone in the organization as he or she strives to enhance the overall performance of the organization.

REFERENCES

Bandura, A. 1977. Self-efficacy: Towards a unifying theory of behavioral change. *Psychological Bulletin*, 80: 286–303.

de Geus, A. 1997. The living company. *Harvard Business Review*, 75 (2): 51–59.

Garvin, D. A. 1995. Leveraging processes for strategic advantage: A roundtable with Xerox's Allaire, USAA's Herres, SmithKline Beecham's Leschly, and Pepsi's Weatherup. *Harvard Business Review*, 73 (5): 76–90.

Hodgetts, R. M., Kuratko, D. F. & Hornsby, J. S. 1999. Quality implementation in small business: Perspectives from the Baldrige Award winners. *S.A.M. Advanced Management Journal*, 64 (1): 37–48.

Kaplan, R. S., & Norton, D. P. 1993. Putting the balanced scorecard to work. *Harvard Business Review*, 71 (5): 134–147.

Kaplan, R. S., & Norton, D. P. 1992. The balanced scorecard: Measures that drive performance. *Harvard Business Review*, 70 (1): 71–79.

Kerr, S. 1975. On the folly of rewarding A, while hoping for B. *Academy of Management Journal*, 18: 769–783.

Lawler, E. E., III, Mohrman, S. A. & Ledford, G. A., Jr. 1992. *Employee involvement and total quality management: Practices and results in Fortune 1,000 companies*. San Francisco: Jossey-Bass.

McAuliffe, P. 1999. Personal interview. December 15, Waterbury, CT.

Meyer, C. 1994. How the right measures help teams excel. *Harvard Business Review*, 72 (3): 95–103.

Meyer, J. P., Paunonen, S. V., Gellatly, I. R., Goffin, R. D. & Jackson, D. N. 1989. Organizational commitment and job performance: It's the nature of commitment that counts. *Journal of Applied Psychology*, 74 (1): 152–156.

Mowday, R. T., Porter, L. W. & Steers, R. M. 1982. *Employee-organization linkages: The psychology of commitment, absenteeism, and turnover*. New York: Academic Press.

Ogilvie, J. R. 1986. The role of human resource management practices in predicting organizational commitment. *Group & Organization Studies*, 11 (4): 335–359.

Plenert, G., & Hibino, S. 1997. *Making innovation happen: Concept management through integration*. Boca Raton, FL: St. Lucie Press.

Reichheld, F. F., & Sasser, W. E., Jr. 1990. Zero defections: Quality comes to services. *Harvard Business Review*, 68 (5): 105–111.

Zemke, R., & Schaaf, D. 1989. *The service edge: 101 companies that profit from customer care*. New York: Plume.

Part III

Emerging Challenges

Chapter 9

Nurturing a Learning Environment

The only irreplaceable capital an organization possesses
is the knowledge and ability of its people. The productivity
of that capital depends on how effectively people share
their competence with those who can use it.

—Andrew Carnegie

As we move into the information age, the capacity of an organization to learn from its experience and the experiences of others is becoming one of the greatest sources of competitive advantage. To take full advantage of this potential asset, however, an organization must be able to collect, analyze, and respond to new information about current and evolving customer needs more quickly than the competition. The secret to making this happen is nurturing a quality culture that supports and rewards learning as well as sharing lessons learned. This chapter focuses on what needs to occur to translate this vision into a competitive reality.

HOW ORGANIZATIONS LEARN

How do you create a learning organization? According to Senge (1990), to become a true learning organization, a firm must develop five disciplines. These disciplines are thinking systemically, promoting personal mastery, sharing mental models, building a shared vision, and encouraging team learning.

In addition to these disciplines, de Geus (1997) has identified three general qualities of the work environment that are also necessary to nurture this type of work environment. First, there must be ample opportunity for social interaction. Second, employees must have the skills and motivation to innovate. Third, there must be systems in place to communicate the results of new findings.

Why are these disciplines and qualities necessary? The answer lies in understanding how individual and group learning differs from organizational learning. Individuals and groups learn from thinking about problems, trying out some potential solutions to the problems, evaluating how well the proposed solution has worked, and then reflecting upon the experience to consolidate lessons learned for the future. In contrast, firms may create elaborate informal and formal databases of information, but since they cannot directly experience work problems or reflect on experiences, they are dependent on individuals and groups embedded deep within the fabric of the organization (Alderfer and Smith, 1982) to be willing and able to communicate their new knowledge to others. Thus, the rate of organizational learning is ultimately dependent on the desire of employees to share their information with others and the capacity of an organization to capture and share this information throughout the organization.

Given this reality, the capacity of an organization to learn will be a function of how well the management of the firm fosters an environment that promotes individual and group experimentation as well as the capturing and sharing of information. In other words, when thinking, doing, evaluating, and reflecting on work are valued, the organization can learn. In the absence of these conditions, little, if any, progress will be made on improving the collective knowledge of the organization.

Thinking

Employees think about problems every day. In learning organizations, however, the nature of that thinking is distinctively different from what occurs in traditional organizations in two important respects. In learning organizations, individuals and teams are encouraged to think about their problems in the context of the larger issues that the organization is trying to address. In other words, specific problems are viewed in the context of larger systemic issues as opposed to being viewed as isolated individual or departmental concerns (Senge, 1990).

Second, in learning organizations it is expected that employees will challenge basic assumptions about how work is being done. Specifically, it is acceptable to ask questions not only about "how we can do it better," but also about whether "we are doing the right things." Thus, in a learning organization there are no "sacred cows" (Argyris, 1994, 1993). This is in sharp contrast to traditional organizations, where questioning standing practices can get an employee or team into serious trouble.

Doing

Employees do work every day. In learning organizations, however, doing work is viewed quite differently than in a traditional organization. In a learning organization, individuals and teams feel truly empowered (Argyris, 1998), where appropriate, to experiment with new approaches to doing assignments. Only by trying out novel solutions can the organization learn to do things better. Sometimes these new approaches work out well, and sometimes they do not. What is important is that employees are willing to try something different. Obviously, this license to experiment is in sharp contrast to the common advice within most traditional organizations that the safest path is just to follow the standard policies and procedures, and you will be fine.

Evaluating

Some form of evaluation usually follows work efforts in all organizations. The scope of the evaluation, however, distinguishes how this task is approached in learning organizations versus more traditional organizations. For example, at the completion of every major project British Petroleum examines the degree to which company assets, technologies, organizational support, and relationships (e.g., with suppliers, partners) were effectively used in the overall process of doing the work (Prokesch, 1997). This rich evaluation is in contrast to more traditional approaches that focus primarily on determining the degree to which target outcomes were achieved.

Reflecting

The most distinctive aspect of how learning organizations approach their work, in contrast to the norms in more traditional organizations, however, is to consciously set aside time after assignments to seriously reflect on what can be learned from the experience. This approach is driven by the recognition that individuals and groups learn best when they actively reflect on their processes and feedback received after working on challenging problems (Marquardt, 1999). Yet, traditional organizations rarely take the time to conduct this type of analysis, and so their opportunities to learn suffer as a result.

BUILDING LEARNING RELATIONSHIPS

Clearly, building partner relationships with employees based on trust and open communication is central to creating a learning organization. Yet, in a true learning organization, the pursuit of new information is not limited to what can be gathered internally. Rather, new ideas are actively sought from anyone who can be trusted and with whom a productive, long-term relationship can be established. Foremost among these learning partners are suppliers, customers, and other organizations.

Suppliers

Building learning relationships for mutual benefit might sound like a new way of enhancing the quality of a firm's products and services. Yet, over a decade ago Deming (1986) talked about the potential value of this approach. Specifically, in his estimation one of the most valuable partners that a firm can have is its suppliers. Indeed, in the entire supply chain few players are more inherently interested in a firm's success than its suppliers. After all, your long-term success is intimately connected to their success.

Yet, many traditional firms insist on keeping an arms-length distance from their suppliers, whom they often call vendors. It is as if they thought their suppliers were out to rob them. True enough, some suppliers are unscrupulous and will take advantage of their customers. On the other hand, if you believe that this is true, then why are you doing business with them in the first place?

Given a chance, good suppliers will strive hard to give you precisely the kinds of goods and services that you need to be successful. However, their ability to deliver is largely a function of how well they know your needs. In the absence of good information a supplier can only guess at what a customer really wants. Building a strong learning relationship with suppliers, therefore, is clearly in the best interests of both parties.

Customers

Is it possible to create a learning relationship with customers? The answer is yes. Indeed, Pine, Peppers, and Rogers (1995) have suggested that if you want to keep customers forever, the best way to do so is to actively create a deep learning relationship with them. Certainly, this is the strategy that Ritz-Carlton Hotels has successfully pursued with the development of its extensive worldwide data base that keeps track of the current and evolving lodging needs of its customers. Andersen Windows, in a somewhat different way, has pursued the same end with its

Knowledge Window, which allows its customers to custom-design and order windows.

Other Firms

Likewise, it is possible to build a learning relationship with other firms. However, these relationships need to be approached with more caution than those with suppliers or customers. Indeed, it is risky to do so without a clear strategic vision of the future for your own firm, a clear understanding of the other firm's culture, and a determination to make the relationship work for the long term.

A clear internal vision is critical because it will allow the organization to know where it is headed and the current status of internal capabilities to meet these future objectives. The best partners will have complementary strengths. Understanding the culture of the potential partner firm is critical because cultural incompatibility will doom many otherwise attractive alliances. Finally, the willingness to commit to a long-term relationship is necessary because, like all relationships, any strategic alliance will demand lots of care and attention.

LEADING A LEARNING ORGANIZATION

While it is possible to collect a great deal of new information from cultivating learning relationships, nothing of much consequence will happen in an organization until this information is used to effectively address the short- and long-term challenges facing the firm. The key to making this happen is often changing the role of management within a firm (Kotter, 1990). Specifically, the role of management must usually change from a primary focus on controlling and directing the activities of others as they solve problems (Kraut, Pedigo, McKenna, and Dunnette, 1989), to that of becoming designers, stewards, and teachers (Senge, 1990).

Making this transition, however, is a substantial undertaking because conventional wisdom places great weight on the need for individuals, work groups, and organizations as a whole to be self-reliant and independent. This is a powerful logic and one that has served many individuals, teams, and firms well in the past. Moreover, once this logic has been ingrained in the thinking of the management team, it will become very resistant to change (Kets de Vries and Miller, 1987).

However, this logic works better in some business environments than others. Specifically, it works best when a firm's markets are relatively stable and fairly fragmented (e.g., regulated utilities). On the other hand, when markets become more turbulent and when the boundaries not only between firms but between whole industries (e.g., communications) start to blur, the value of this logic as the dominant operating philosophy becomes more suspect (Drucker, 1994).

More precisely, in turbulent and rapidly changing markets, independence and competitiveness are still viable goals. However, there is also a greater need to recognize that collaboration aimed at enhancing the rate of organizational learning, when done well and properly, is equally important (Kanter, 1994, 1989). In other words, departments within an organization must come to recognize that valuable lessons can be learned as readily from the experiences of others outside the department as well as from experiences within the department.

Grupo Financiero Serfin

The value of adopting this learning perspective was clearly seen in the recent experience of Grupo Financiero Serfin, one of Mexico's largest banks. In the wake of Mexico's 1994 currency crisis, management had to decide what to do with a growing number of loan defaults. Over the years, the bank's management had developed a standard process for negotiating loan workouts. In these situations the loan negotiators sat down with each debtor and traded concessions around what would be repaid, when, and under what conditions. These negotiations were backed up with occasional threats of legal action. Unfortunately, given the severity of the economic crisis, this traditional approach to resolving problem loans was proving to be unsuccessful in improving the position of the bank's overall portfolio (Ertel, 1999).

In the past, management would have resorted to encouraging the loan negotiators to just stick with the old procedure and try harder. This time, management decided to try another approach. Specifically, it decided to look at loan negotiation not as a series of discrete events but rather as an institutional capability.

To improve the firm's negotiating capability, it began by improving the bank's negotiation training curriculum by putting trainees in real-world, simulated situations. Then, it took its effort to a whole new level. The bank's financial analysts closely inspected each workout case to clarify the bank's interests in it and its priority as a case, developed an understanding of each debtor's interests, prepared a set of creative options for resolving the case, and then assessed the bank's and the customer's alternatives for seeking a reasonable solution. This rich analysis then became a blueprint for how the negotiations should proceed.

In addition, the bank went on to create a categorization scheme based on rating each debtor on four factors. These factors included the debtor's ability to repay the loan, the quality of the relationship, the quality of its collateral, and the quality of the bank's best alternative solution. This categorization scheme, in turn, suggested the most preferred negotiation strategy. For example, finding that a debtor had a strained relationship with the bank but good collateral and ability to pay would suggest that an attempt to strengthen the underlying relationship was the most prudent course of action.

To further help the negotiation teams implement their strategies, the company set up a system for sharing best practices. Specifically, negotiators from five workout divisions within the bank identified their 20 most difficult cases. Then, working with a negotiation coach, they analyzed what had happened to date on each of the cases and how best to proceed. These sessions led to the identification of lessons learned that could be shared throughout the bank. This information was also used to enhance the categorization scheme. As a result of this significant learning effort, the negotiators became much more creative, and today Serfin's workout divisions are considered to be the best in the country (Ertel, 1999).

Changing Organizational Strategies

To make full use of the information gathered from a host of learning relationships, however, may require that organizations make even broader changes than occurred at Grupo Financiero Serfin. Pine, Peppers, and Rogers (1995) have identified four key areas that are likely to be impacted. First, a company's overall information strategy might need to change from a focus on storing static information about customers, to creating opportunities for initiating dialogues with customers and remembering their preferences through the use of interactive technologies such as electronic kiosks, on-line services, and database-driven mail.

Second, an organization's production/delivery strategy may need to change from a focus on meeting internal production schedules, to determining customers' needs as precisely as possible and then organizing the production process to meet the needs as efficiently as possible.

Third, the traditional organizational marketing strategy of pushing products and services into the market may need to be replaced by customer managers to build better learning relationships with customers and by capability managers to ensure that orders can be filled in a timely fashion.

Finally, a firm's overall assessment strategy might need to evolve from a focus on evaluating the success of a short-term product or service offering, to a focus on the lifetime value from a customer relationship. In this worldview, customer share (i.e., how much of a customer's business is going to the firm) and customer sacrifice (i.e., the gap between what each customer truly wants and needs and what the company can supply) will become more relevant measures of organizational performance.

In summary, nurturing a learning environment is emerging as one of the great challenges for firms in their quest to improve quality because it can dramatically enhance the improvement of the quality of products and services that a firm can offer to its customers. Being successful in this quest, however, will be a function of establishing a disciplined approach and a learning environment aimed at fostering learning throughout the organization.

REFERENCES

Alderfer, C. P., & Smith, K. K. 1982. Studying intergroup relations embedded in organizations. *Administrative Science Quarterly*, 27 (1): 35–65.

Argyris, C. 1998. Empowerment: The emperor's new clothes. *Harvard Business Review*, 76 (3): 98–105.

Argyris, C. 1994. Good communication that blocks learning. *Harvard Business Review*, 72 (4): 77–85.

Argyris, C. 1993. *Knowledge for action*. San Francisco: Jossey-Bass.

de Gues, A. 1997. The living company. *Harvard Business Review*, 75 (2): 51–59.

Deming, W. E. 1986. *Out of the crisis*. Cambridge: MIT Center for Advanced Engineering Study.

Drucker, P. 1994. The theory of the business. *Harvard Business Review*, 72 (5): 95–104.

Ertel, D. 1999. Turning negotiation into a corporate capability. *Harvard Business Review*, 77 (3): 55–56, 58, 60, 62, 64, 66, 68–70.

Kanter, R. M. 1994. Collaborative advantage: The art of alliances. *Harvard Business Review*, 72 (4): 96–108.

Kanter, R. M. 1989. Becoming PALs: Pooling, allying, and linking across companies. *Academy of Management Executive*, 3 (3): 183–193.

Kets de Vries, M. F. R., & Miller, D. 1987. *The neurotic organization: Diagnosing and changing counterproductive styles of management*. San Francisco: Jossey-Bass.

Kotter, J. P. 1990. *A force for change: How leadership differs from management*. New York: Free Press.

Kraut, A. I., Pedigo, P. R., McKenna, D. D. & Dunnette, M. D. 1989. The role of the manager: What's really important in different management jobs. *Academy of Management Executive*, 3 (4): 286–293.

Marquardt, M. J. 1999. *Action learning in action: Transforming problems and people for world-class organizational learning*. Palo Alto, CA: Davies-Black.

Pine, J. B. II, Peppers, D. & Rogers, M. 1995. Do you want to keep your customers forever? *Harvard Business Review*, 73 (2): 36–47.

Prokesch, S. E. 1997. Unleashing the power of learning: An interview with British Petroleum's John Browne. *Harvard Business Review*, 75 (5): 146–148, 150, 152–158, 160, 162, 164, 166, 168.

Senge, P. M. 1990. *The fifth discipline: The art and practice of the learning organization.* New York: Doubleday.

Chapter 10

Moving Forward

In the future, the only source of competitive advantage for companies will be their superior ability to learn and change.

—Arie de Geus, 1997

As discussed throughout this book, the quest for quality improvement is a journey without an end. Each advancement in our understanding of how to provide higher-quality goods and services provides a platform for even greater enhancements. Where are the breakthroughs coming today that will help to establish the standards for tomorrow? Two of the most exciting advances are coming from interrelated areas. One is the demonstrated ability of firms to attain six sigma levels of precision in the production of goods and services. The other area is the growing interest in improving the quality of information, which is critical for making better decisions about, and delivering ever more, value to customers.

SIX SIGMA—NEW LEVELS OF PRECISION

Sigma is a statistical term that measures the extent to which a process deviates from perfection. Having this type of measure is invaluable to firms interested in improving their quality because it provides a universal, standard measure to allow for process quality comparisons within a firm, across firms within the same industry, and even across industries.

At the present time, most firms are operating at around a three-sigma level of precision. This translates to 66,807 defects per million opportunities to perform a process correctly. To reach six-sigma levels of quality, however, a firm can make no more than 3.4 defects per million opportunities. Clearly, hitting this goal means that a firm is approaching virtual perfection and Phil Crosby's (1979) dream goal of zero defects.

Motorola Reaches Six Sigma First

For many decades attaining six-sigma levels of quality was viewed like running a three-minute mile—a noble goal but probably unattainable. That is, until in the early 1980s when Bob Galvin, then chairman of Motorola, challenged his company to achieve a ten-fold improvement in performance during a five-year period of time. This challenge sparked a drive among the firm's executives to aggressively identify ways to cut waste from the firm.

Meanwhile, deep in the organization an engineer named Bill Smith was conducting a study of the correlation between a product's field life and how often that product had to be repaired. What he discovered would prove to be the key to unlocking the secret of how to reach six sigma levels of quality. Specifically, he found that if a product was assembled error-free, the product rarely failed in the field. The secret to six-sigma performance, therefore, was not in making perfect products but rather in creating a perfect quality *system* (Harry, 1998).

To build a better quality system obviously meant that an integrated quality strategy would need to be developed for the whole firm (Pyzdek, 1999b). After Motorola's strategy was in place, it reached the goal of six sigma in eight years.

How was this goal reached? The secret was to organize efforts to simultaneously achieve breakthroughs in the measurement, analysis, improvement, and control of business processes led by rigorously trained six-sigma "black belts." These individuals are highly skilled in number crunching, advanced problem-solving tools and techniques, project management, and team dynamics. Their training consists of comprehensive knowledge of techniques such as process mapping, measurement-system analysis, graphical analysis, capability analysis, hypothesis analysis, regression analysis, analysis of variance, supply-chain management, design of experiments, mistake proofing, statistical process control, failure-mode-effects analysis, and gage repeatability and reproducibility.

General Electric Sets Higher Standards

In 1995 Jack Welch, chairman of General Electric (GE) decided that if Motorola could produce six-sigma levels of quality, then so could his firm. Moreover, if it took Motorola eight years to get there, GE could do it in five (Conlin, 1998). Accordingly, Welch launched his companywide six-sigma program in 1995 with 200 projects supported by intensive training. In the next year, he moved to 3,000 projects with additional training. In 1997 GE was pursuing 6,000 projects, and even more training was added.

The results of this effort have been impressive. In 1997 alone, six-sigma projects delivered $320 million in productivity gains and profits, which was more than double Welch's original goal of $150 million. Moreover, these gains are not just in manufacturing but throughout the entire organization (Pyzdek, 1999a). Based on these returns, it is little wonder that Welch has now challenged everyone in the firm to become a "quality lunatic."

Today, GE has nearly 4,000 full-time, fully trained black belts and master black belts. In addition, there are over 60,000 green belt, part-time project leaders who have completed at least one six-sigma project. The number grows every day.

Citibank

Six-sigma quality might be possible to attain in a manufacturing environment, but could it also be achieved in a service company? Citibank decided to try. In 1997 it hired Motorola University Consulting and Training Services to teach six-sigma defect reduction and cycle time reduction to its employees. From May 1997 to October 1997 more than 650 senior managers were trained. Between November 1997 and the end of 1998 another 7,500 employees were trained by senior manager-led teams. By early 1999 an additional 92,000 employees worldwide were trained.

This investment has already yielded significant returns. For example, in the Private Bank—Western Hemisphere group, internal call backs have been reduced by 80%, external calls have declined by 85%, and credit-processing time has been slashed by 50%. In the Global Equipment Finance division, the six-sigma and cycle time reduction effort has reduced the credit decision cycle by 67%, from three days to one. Likewise, in the Copeland Companies subsidiary, these tools have improved the accuracy of financial statements to 100% during a four-month period of time and reduced statement-processing time from 28 to 15 days (Rucker, 1999).

INFORMATION QUALITY—NEW FRONTIER FOR IMPROVEMENT

The focus of the discussion throughout this book has been on how to improve the quality of products and services. It is clear from this discussion that enhanced approaches to attaining this goal are being developed on a host of fronts. As we move into the information age, however, another question is surfacing. Is it possible that the next quality revolution will focus not on products and services per se but on improving the quality of information that drives the production process itself?

Albrecht (1999), among others, believes that this is exactly where the next breakthroughs will come because while information is proliferating at an exponential rate, it is not always very good information. For example, while the United States has the reputation for providing the best medical care in the world, the American Medical Association estimates that more than 120,000 Americans die every year because of errors in diagnosis, treatment, or medication. Likewise, retailers are proud of their new point-of-sale price scanners, but several recent studies have revealed that they may register incorrect prices as often as 1-3% of the time. Closer to home, about 20-30% of the calls to the Internal Revenue Service are abandoned by callers due to long wait times, and as many as 25% of the callers are receiving incorrect information about tax rules.

Two major forces are at work, however, that should lead to continued improvements in the quality of information. One force is the development of new technologies that can speed the facilitation and manipulation of information. The other major force is improving ways of utilizing the extraordinary capacity that is being created (Zuboff, 1988).

Hardware and Software Keep Getting Better

Every day the capacity of computer hardware to handle larger volumes of information in less time is increasing. What is more important, however, is that these machines are being designed to facilitate *interactive communication*, and it is through the use of rapidly expanding interactive technologies such as electronic kiosks, on-line (e.g., AOL, Amazon.com), and database-driven mail services (e.g., Waldenbooks) that the very essence of the supplier-customer relationship is being redefined (Pine, Peppers, and Rogers, 1995).

At the same time, we are starting to understand that our computer software applications must be designed to fulfill different functions depending on what issue(s) they are intended to address and who will be using them. For example, some software packages need to provide conformance to clearly defined specifications (e.g., accounting applications). Others applications need to be user-friendly (e.g., internal customer databases). Meanwhile, yet others must be able to constantly evolve through experience with users (e.g., e-commerce) (Prahalad and Krishnan, 1999).

The Devil Is in the Details of Implementation

The good news, therefore, is that our technological prowess grows steadily every day. The bad news is that technology alone will be insufficient to improve the quality of information feeding organizations throughout the world. Only when firms come to accept what we have known for a long time (Mann and Williams, 1960), that improvement will be a function of the technology, processes, and people involved in doing the work, will the full potential of this revolution be realized (Motiwalla and Fairfield-Sonn, 1998).

More precisely, in addition to buying more advanced technology, at a minimum, we will also need to find ways to more systematically improve software applications (Bloodworth, 1999) and how they work together (Prahalad and Krishnan, 1999). Better yet, organizations must move from viewing information technology as the domain of the IT department, to an enterprise-wide source of process improvement (Harkness and Kettinger, 1996). Finally, organizations must create a culture where the pursuit of better information is just how business gets done (Mereau and Labbe, 1997).

In summary, as we move forward, two of the most exciting quality frontiers that will present great challenges but also hold the greatest promise of rewards are to improve the precision of firm processes and the quality of information going into and coming out of them. Meeting these twin challenges will require extraordinary technological skills but also the creation and nurturing of organizational cultures that cherish and reward continuous improvement and organizational learning.

REFERENCES

Albrecht, K. 1999. The next quality revolution: Information. *Quality Digest*, 19 (6): 30–32.

Bloodworth, D. 1999. A systematic way to improve software. *American Banker*, 164 (111): 9.

Conlin, M. 1998. Revealed at last: The secret of Jack Welch's success. *Forbes*, 161 (2): 44.

Crosby, P.B. 1979. *Quality is free: The art of making quality certain*. New York: McGraw-Hill.

Harkness, W. L., & Kettinger, W. J. 1996. Sustaining process improvement and innovation in the information services function. *MIS Quarterly*, 20 (3): 349–369.

Harry, M. 1998. Six sigma: A breakthrough strategy for profitability. *Quality Progress*, May: 60–65.

Mann, F. C., & Williams, L. K. 1960. Observations on the dynamics of a change to electronic data-processing equipment. *Administrative Science Quarterly*, (3): 217–256.

Mereau, P., & Labbe, E. 1997. Practices and technology transfer in quality and information technology. *Human Systems Management*, 16 (3): 195–201.

Motiwalla, L., & Fairfield-Sonn, J. W. 1998. Measuring the impact of expert systems. *Journal of Business and Economic Studies*, 4 (2): 1–17.

Pine, J. B. II, Peppers, D. & Rogers, M. 1995. Do you want to keep your customers forever? *Harvard Business Review*, 73 (2): 36–47.

Prahalad, C. K., & Krishnan, M. S. 1999. The new meaning of quality in the information age. *Harvard Business Review*, 77 (5): 109–118.

Pyzdek, T., 1999a. Six sigma is primarily a management program. *Quality Digest*, 19 (6): 26.

Pyzdek, T., 1999b. The value of six sigma. *Quality Digest*, 19 (12): 20.

Rucker, R. 1999. Six sigma at Citibank. *Quality Digest*, 19 (12): 28–32.

Zuboff, S. 1988. *In the age of the smart machine: The future of work and power*. New York: Basic Books.

Chapter 11

Summary and Conclusions

All happy families resemble one another, but each
unhappy family is unhappy in its own way.

—Leon Tolstoy

The intent of this book was to provide some useful insights into,
and practical ideas about, how to build a quality organization. To
describe the full scope of this task, we examined three critical
aspects of the quality journey. First, we looked at the importance of
creating the proper mind-set to begin and sustain the effort. Then,
we explored several vital, interrelated steps that need to be taken
to make it happen. We concluded by exploring some of the quality
challenges that are emerging on the horizon. As we end this
discussion, it becomes apparent that Tolstoy's observation about
families is equally true about quality organizations. In the end,
they all resemble each other. What links them in a common bond
are the understanding and belief that the pursuit of continuous
improvement is a richly rewarding way of doing business for
customers, employees, and stakeholders writ large. Working from
this basic assumption, each organization's quality journey will be
unique, but the ultimate goal of trying to get better every day in a

host of different ways is the same, and this is the source of its happiness.

IMPROVING QUALITY

To improve quality, you need to know not only what to do but also *how* to do it. In other words, there are more and less effective ways to make the transition to a continuous work improvement environment a reality. Unfortunately, many firms have tried to make the change, and the effort stalled or failed. When this happened, management may have concluded that this "quality stuff" is just a fad and that we should just go back to our old ways of doing business. This is an unfortunate conclusion to draw because concerns about quality will not go away. On the contrary, the pressures to enhance quality are mounting. Only those firms that are clear about their core values and deeply committed to the unrelenting pursuit of continuous quality improvement will be profitable and thrive over the long term.

A better response is to ask, What went wrong with our implementation process? By looking at a wide range of firms that have successfully implemented quality improvement efforts, common patterns emerge. These patterns suggest that Pareto's 20:80 rule holds true in this arena as in so many areas of life. That is, a vital few activities explain most of the observed positive results, and an endless array of "little" efforts, while helpful, will not give much of a payback. So, begin with basic, high-impact activities, and, as time and resources permit, follow up with efforts that will have an impact on the margins.

What are the vital few activities? As discussed in Part I of this book, the process needs to begin with a solid foundation. That means that quality improvement must become an integral part of a firm's vision, culture, and strategic management systems. Moreover, this work can be done only by the senior management team because unlike technical change, which can be delegated, building the foundation for a quality effort demands a unified, committed, top-down effort. No amount of good intention or special effort in localized areas of the organization will ever make this happen.

Once the senior management team is on board, and the foundation is in place, then the focus needs to shift to drilling the effort down into the organization. This effort must be pursued in a number of ways. First, quality improvement has to become a strategic priority. That is, while a firm's strategies will change over time, they must always be formulated in light of the question of how they will contribute to the enhancement of the overall quality of the organization's products and services. Likewise, a conscious effort needs to be made to make the organization truly customer-focused. In other words, all the firm's systems, processes, and procedures must also be aimed at improving external and internal customer satisfaction and taking action to improve results in this area.

Next, a structure for organizing, coordinating, deploying, and supporting process improvement teams must be created and continually refined. As discussed, there are many ways to structure these teams, but the "best" structure is always one that reflects, to the greatest extent possible, dominant quality values around employee empowerment, participation, and making decisions for the good of the whole organization. This value-driven alignment is important to the success of the effort because process improvement teams are truly the engine that will drive the organization, and the structure needs to feel right to promote maximum participation in them.

At the same time, it must be recognized that many employees will not actively engage in any of these change efforts, regardless of the structure, unless they are recognized and rewarded for their efforts. Accordingly, the senior management team must ensure that employees can easily see how involvement in the effort will lead both to long-term personal and professional growth as well as to short-term recognition and rewards.

LESSONS LEARNED

What insights can be drawn from this book about how to build a quality organization? Seven major points are summarized next for your consideration.

It Takes Strong Visionary Leaders to Build a Quality Organization

To transform a traditional, hierarchical organization into a process-oriented, continuous improvement workplace requires strong visionary leadership for one basic reason. Many managers, supervisors, and employees who grew up in traditional hierarchical organizations view quality management as softhearted and softheaded. They wonder how anyone in his or her right mind would give up control over people and budgets to embrace this new "empowerment" thing. Accordingly, they will resist this new philosophy of management and its associated practices until they become convinced of its merits. Yet, without their full support nothing of much consequence will come from the effort.

In reality, the perception of these managers, supervisors, and employees is wrong. In quality organizations there is abundant concern for adequately controlling people and budgets. What is different is that a new and more powerful form of control is also possible. That control is around making processes work more effectively, which, in turn, can lead to dramatic improvements in performance. However, since perception becomes reality, leaders must provide a vision for a new future that clearly conveys that there is a better way of doing business. Only visionary leaders will be able to make this happen, and this is tough work.

You Need to Adopt a Long-Term Perspective

Quality improvement is not a quick-fix solution to an organization's problems. While it is possible to get some short-term returns by attacking so-called low-hanging-fruit opportunities, significant returns for an investment in quality improvement will come only when you adopt a long-term perspective. This is because experience has shown that it may well take up to a year before the benefits from a typical effort start to exceed the start-up costs involved in getting the effort under way. Moreover, it may take 3 to 5 years before the effort becomes firmly established and perhaps as long as 10 years to become completely accepted as the new way of doing business throughout the organization.

However, rest assured that the returns for your investment will grow each year in new and unexpected ways. This is the beauty of pursuing quality in a serious way.

Creating a Quality Culture Is the Key to Success

Considerable time, effort, and passion will be necessary to make this endeavor successful because major quality gains are ultimately contingent upon establishing a quality culture that values and rewards contributions made to the improvement of the functioning of the whole organization. Since culture change demands that not only behaviors but also beliefs must change, this effort will obviously take time. As this culture starts to take shape, however, your return for investments in training employees in the technical tools and techniques of process improvement will grow exponentially.

Begin with a Model and Drill It Down into the Organization

To be successful in creating a quality culture within a firm, you need to have a clear road map for the journey. Having an overall plan of attack is critical because fostering cultural change is one of the most complex and challenging organizational development efforts that a firm will ever attempt. Accordingly, it is easy to get lost along the way, and getting sidetracked will cost you valuable time and money.

Fortunately, it is not necessary to create a road map from whole cloth, although you can if you want to. There is already abundant guidance on how to make this journey more efficient and rewarding. Foremost among the sources of help with the journey are a well-articulated framework and guidelines provided by the quality experts who have worked for over a decade to structure and clarify the Malcolm Baldrige Quality Award program. Working with this or another model will help everyone in the organization to see both the big picture of where the organization as a whole is going as well as the role of each individual, team, and department within the larger scheme of things.

Trust Your Intuition, but Run the Numbers

To make significant progress on the quality journey, it is critical for members of the organization to believe that long-term benefits will be forthcoming as a result of their commitment to this way of managing the firm. At the same time, it is equally important to become highly disciplined in running the numbers to ensure that near-term progress is, in fact, being made on the quality agenda.

Running the numbers, however, does not mean just establishing statistical process controls, although these are very important. It means establishing, monitoring, and taking action based on the results of a robust set of performance indicators aimed at revealing how well the organization as a whole is progressing on the quality journey. Specifically, these measures need to combine information on both lagging (e.g., financial, operational) and leading (e.g., customer satisfaction, innovation and learning) indicators of performance. Moreover, the results on these performance indicators need to be widely shared throughout the organization on a frequent basis and intimately linked to the firm's recognition and reward system. In this way, performance data can help the organization to make better decisions and add fuel to the drive toward excellence.

Everyone Must Be Able to Share Equitably in the Rewards from the Effort

One of the fundamental principles of quality improvement is to optimize the functioning of the whole system. Over the long term this philosophy will be accepted by employees only if it also becomes clear that the organization is intent on likewise sharing the fruits of the effort with everyone, to the degree that he or she has helped to make the firm prosper. Thus, if senior management takes the lion's share of the rewards, the effort will fail. On the other hand, if everyone shares equally in the rewards, the effort will also fail. The only way to make a quality improvement effort succeed is to provide an opportunity for everyone to share in the benefits from the effort and then ensure that recognition and rewards are equitably distributed based on visible contributions to the well-being of the firm.

Quality Improvement Is a Journey without an End

Quality improvement is not about reaching a final destination. Rather, the quest for quality is a way of life. It is a worldview and a philosophy of management that can make each day into another adventure and challenge. Passing through one door leads to another room of opportunity, and the process never ends.

In summary, this book has highlighted not only what you need to do to build a quality organization but also how to make continuous quality improvement just "the way we do business." By working with the general framework detailed here, every organization can improve the quality of the products and services that it delivers. Making this transition happen will be a function of doing a few things very well and being committed to the process for the long haul. Each of the focal activities discussed in this book can provide you with additional leverage to improve the quality efforts of your organization. At the same time, a weakness in any of these areas will limit the overall ability of your organization to deliver on its promise of improving the quality of its products and services.

Like spokes on a wheel, each of these structural activities helps to determine the overall strength of the whole effort. Yet, the strength of a wheel is also determined by the open space between each spoke. That open space is a firm's culture. Thus, to fashion a strong wheel, attention must be equally focused on both the spokes and the open space between them.

In conclusion, quality improvement is not a quick-fix strategy. To be successful, a continuous improvement effort must become deeply embedded in the fabric of the organization, and that takes time, determination, and dedicated resources. On the other hand, it is also the best course to pursue if you want to be around to meet the challenges of the future. Good luck on your quality journey.

Selected Bibliography

BOOKS

Aguayo, R. 1990. *Dr. Deming: The American who taught the Japanese about quality.* New York: Simon & Schuster.

Argyris, C. 1993. *Knowledge for action.* San Francisco: Jossey-Bass.

Baldrige National Quality Program 2000. *Criteria for performance excellence.* Washington, D.C.: NIST.

Bauman, R. P., Jackson, P. & Lawrence, J. T. 1997. *From promise to performance: A journey of transformation at SmithKline Beecham.* Boston: Harvard Business School Press.

Bower, J. L., Bartlett, C. A., Uyterhoeven, H. E. R. & Walton, R. E. 1995. *Business policy: Managing strategic processes.* 8th ed. Chicago: Irwin.

Buono, A. F., & Bowditch, J. L. 1989. *The human side of mergers and acquisitions.* San Francisco: Jossey-Bass.

Buzzell, R. D., & Gale, B. T. 1987. *The PIMS (profit impact of market strategy) principles: Linking strategy to performance.* New York: Free Press.

Camp, R.C. 1995. *Business process benchmarking: Finding and implementing best practices.* Milwaukee: ASQC Press.

Camp, R. C. 1989. *Benchmarking: The search for industry best practices that lead to superior performance.* Milwaukee: Quality Press.

Collins, J. C., & Porras, J. I. 1994. *Built to last: Successful practices of visionary companies.* New York: Harper Business.

Covey, S. R. 1989. *The 7 habits of highly effective people.* New York: Simon & Schuster.

Crosby, P. B. 1988. *The eternally successful organization: The art of corporate wellness.* New York: McGraw-Hill.

Crosby, P. B. 1979. *Quality is free: The art of making quality certain.* New York: McGraw-Hill.

Crownover, D., Bush, L. & Darrouzet, J. 1999. *Take it to the next level: A story of the quest for quality and the Malcolm Baldrige Award.* Dallas, TX: NextLevel Press.

Davis, S. M. 1984. *Managing corporate culture.* Cambridge, MA: Ballinger.

Deal, T. E., & Kennedy, A. A. 1982. *Corporate cultures: The rites and rituals of corporate life.* Reading, MA: Addison-Wesley.

Deming, W. E. 1986. *Out of the crisis.* Cambridge: MIT Center for Advanced Engineering Study.

Deming, W. E. 1982. *Quality, productivity, and competitive position.* Cambridge: MIT Center for Advanced Engineering Study.

Finkelstein, S., & Hambrick, D. C. 1996. *Strategic leadership: Top executives and their effects on organizations.* Minneapolis: West.

Fishbein, M. & Ajzen, I. 1975. *Beliefs, attitude, intention, and behavior: An introduction to theory and research.* Reading, MA: Addison-Wesley.

Galbraith, J. R., Lawler, E. E. III, & Associates. 1993. *Organizing for the future: The new logic for managing complex organizations.* San Francisco: Jossey-Bass.

Gale, B. T. 1994. *Managing customer value.* New York: Free Press.

Hackman, J. R. (Ed.). 1990. *Groups that work (and those that don't).* San Francisco: Jossey-Bass.

Hamel, G., & Prahalad, C. K. 1994. *Competing for the future.* Boston: Harvard Business School Press.

Hax, A. C., & Majluf, N. S. 1991. *The strategy concept and process: A pragmatic approach.* Englewood Cliffs, NJ: Prentice-Hall.

Hayes, B. E. 1992. *Measuring customer satisfaction: Development and use of questionnaires.* Milwaukee: ASQC Quality Press.

Heifetz, R. A. 1994. *Leadership without easy answers.* Cambridge: Harvard University Press.

Herzberg, F., Mausner, B., & Synderman, B. 1959. *The motivation to work.* New York: John Wiley & Sons.

Juran, J. M. 1988. *Juran on planning for quality.* New York: Free Press.

Kaplan, R. S., & Atkinson, A. A. 1998. *Advanced management accounting.* Upper Saddle River, NJ: Prentice-Hall.

Katzenbach, J. R., & Smith, D. K. 1993. *The wisdom of teams: Creating the high-performance organization.* Boston: Harvard Business School Press.

Kets de Vries, M. F. R., & Miller, D. 1987. *The neurotic organization: Diagnosing and changing counterproductive styles of management.* San Francisco: Jossey-Bass.

Kilmann, R. H. 1989. *Managing beyond the quick fix: A completely integrated program for creating and maintaining organizational success.* San Francisco: Jossey-Bass.

Kinlaw, D. C. 1989. *Coaching for commitment: Managerial strategies for obtaining superior performance.* San Diego: Pfeiffer.

Kotler, P., Jatusripitak, S., & Maesincee, S. 1997. *The marketing of nations.* New York: Free Press.

Kotter, J. P. 1990. *A force for change: How leadership differs from management.* New York: Free Press.

Kotter, J. P., & Heskett, J. L. 1992. *Corporate culture and performance.* New York: Free Press.

Krueger, R. A. 1994. *Focus groups: A practical guide for applied research.* 2nd ed. Thousand Oaks, CA: Sage.

Lawler, E. E. III, Mohrman, S. A., and Ledford, G. A., Jr. 1992. *Employee involvement and total quality management: Practices and results in Fortune 1,000 companies.* San Francisco: Jossey-Bass.

Levinson, H. 1989. *Designing and managing your career.* Boston: Harvard Business School Press.

Marquardt, M. J. 1999. *Action learning in action: Transforming problems and people for world-class organizational learning.* Palo Alto, CA: Davies-Black.

McQuarrie, E. F. 1996. *The market research toolbox: A concise guide for beginners.* Thousand Oaks, CA: Sage.

McQuarrie, E. F. 1993. *Customer visits: Building a better market focus.* Newbury Park, CA: Sage.

Miller, A. F., Jr., & Mattson, R. T. 1989. *The truth about you.* Berkeley, CA: Ten Speed Press.

Mohrman, S. A., Cohen, S. G., & Mohrman, A. M., Jr. 1995. *Designing team-based organizations: New forms for knowledge work.* San Francisco: Jossey-Bass.

Morgan, G. 1986. *Images of organization.* Beverly Hills, CA: Sage.

Mowday, R. T., Porter, L. W., & Steers, R. M. 1982. *Employee-organization linkages: The psychology of commitment, absenteeism, and turnover.* New York: Academic Press.

Nader, R. 1966. *Unsafe at any speed.* New York: Pocket Books.

Nanus, B. 1992. *Visionary leadership.* San Francisco: Jossey-Bass.

Neuhauser, P. C. 1993. *Corporate legends and lore.* New York: McGraw-Hill.

Ott, J. S. 1989. *The organizational culture perspective.* Chicago: Irwin.

Peters, T. J., & Waterman, R. H., Jr. 1982. *In search of excellence: Lessons from America's best-run companies.* New York: Harper & Row.

Plenert, G., & Hibino, S. 1997. *Making innovation happen: Concept management through integration.* Boca Raton, FL: St. Lucie Press.

Porter, M. E. 1985. *Competitive advantage: Creating and sustaining superior performance.* New York: Free Press.

Porter, M. E. 1980. *Competitive strategy: Techniques for analyzing industries and competitiors.* New York: Free Press.

Schein, E. H. 1985. *Organizational culture and leadership.* San Francisco: Jossey-Bass.

Senge, P. M. 1990. *The fifth discipline: The art and practice of the learning organization.* New York: Doubleday.

Sinclair, U. 1906. *The jungle.* New York: New American Library.

Slywotzky, A. J., & Morrison, D. J. 1997. *The profit zone: How strategic business design will lead you to tomorrow's profits.* New York: Random House.

Treacy, M., & Wiersema, F. 1995. *The discipline of market leaders.* Reading, MA: Addison-Wesley.

ARTICLES

Albrecht, K. 1999. The next quality revolution: Information. *Quality Digest,* 19 (6): 30–32.

Alderfer, C. P., & Smith, K. K. 1982. Studying intergroup relations embedded in organizations. *Administrative Science Quarterly,* 27 (1): 35–65.

Argyris, C. 1998. Empowerment: The emperor's new clothes. *Harvard Business Review,* 76 (3): 98–105.

Argyris, C. 1994. Good communication that blocks learning. *Harvard Business Review,* 72 (4): 77–85.

Ashkenas, R. N., DeMonaco, L. J., & Francis, S. C. 1998. Making the deal real: How GE Capital integrates acquisitions. *Harvard Business Review,* 76 (1): 165–178.

Bandura, A. 1977. Self-efficacy: Towards a unifying theory of behavioral change. *Psychological Bulletin,* 80: 286–303.

Barney, J. 1995. Looking inside for competitive advantage. *Academy of Management Executive,* 9 (4): 49–61.

Brenneman, G. 1998. Right away and all at once: How we saved Continental. *Harvard Business Review,* 76 (5): 162–179.

Byrne, J. A. 1993. The horizontal corporation. *Business Week,* December 20: 77–81.

Carsky, M. L., Dickinson, R. A., & Canedy, C. R. III. 1998. The evolution of quality in consumer goods. *Journal of Macromarketing,* 18 (2): 132–143.

Charan, R., & Colvin, G. 1999. Why CEOs fail. *Fortune,* 139 (12): 68–72, 74, 76, 78.

Cole, R. E., Bacdayan, P., & White, B. J. 1993. Quality, participation, and competitiveness. *California Management Review,* 35 (3): 68–81.

Collins, J. C., & Porras, J. I. 1996. Building your company's vision. *Harvard Business Review,* 74 (5): 65–77.

DeBaylo, P. 1999. Ten reasons why the Baldrige model works. *The Journal for Quality & Participation,* 1: 1–5.

de Geus, A. 1997. The living company. *Harvard Business Review*, 75 (2): 51–59.

de Geus, A. 1988. Planning as learning. *Harvard Business Review*, 66 (2): 70–74.

Denison, D. R., Hart, S. L., & Kahn, J. A. 1996. From chimneys to cross-functional teams: Developing and validating a diagnostic model. *Academy of Management Journal*, 39 (4): 1005–1023.

Drucker, P. F. 1999. Managing oneself. *Harvard Business Review*, 77 (2): 65–74.

Drucker, P. F. 1994. The theory of the business. *Harvard Business Review*, 72 (5): 95–104.

Ertel, D. 1999. Turning negotiation into a corporate capability. *Harvard Business Review*, 77 (3): 55–56, 58, 60, 62, 64, 66, 68–70.

Fairfield-Sonn, J. W. 1999. Influence of context on process improvement teams: Leadership from a distance. *Journal of Business & Economic Studies*, 5 (2): 61–80.

Fairfield-Sonn, J. W. 1993. Moving beyond vision: Fostering cultural change in a bureaucracy. *Journal of Organizational Change Management*, 6 (5): 43–55.

Fairfield-Sonn, J. W. 1984. What is your organization's I.Q.? *Municipal Management*, 6 (4): 127–131.

Fairfield-Sonn, J.W., and Lacey, N. 1996. Prospects for small business in Poland's future. *Managerial Finance*, 22 (10): 64–72.

Friedman, S. D., Christensen, P., & DeGroot, J. 1998. Work and life: The end of the zero-sum game. *Harvard Business Review*, 76 (6): 119–129.

Garvin, D. A. 1995. Leveraging processes for strategic advantage: A roundtable with Xerox's Allaire, USAA's Herres, SmithKline Beecham's Leschly, and Pepsi's Weatherup. *Harvard Business Review*, 73 (5): 77–90.

Garvin, D. A. 1987. Competing on eight dimensions of quality. *Harvard Business Review*, 65 (6): 101–109.

Hambrick, D. C., & Mason, P. A. 1984. Upper echelons: The organization as a reflection of its top managers. *Academy of Management Review*, 9 (2): 193–206.

Hamel, G., & Prahalad, C. K. 1994. Competing for the future. *Harvard Business Review*, 72 (4): 122–128.

Hardaker, M., & Ward, B. K. 1987. How to make a team work. *Harvard Business Review*, 65 (6): 112–117.

Harkness, W. L., & Kettinger, W. J. 1996. Sustaining process improvement and innovation in the information services function. *MIS Quarterly*, 20 (3): 349–369.

Harry, M. 1998. Six sigma: A breakthrough strategy for profitability. *Quality Progress*, May: 60–65.

Hart, C. W. L., Heskett, J. L., & Sasser, W. E., Jr. 1990. The profitable art of service recovery. *Harvard Business Review*, 68 (4): 148–156.

Heifetz, R. 1998. Walking the fine line of leadership. *The Journal for Quality and Participation*, 21 (1): 8–14.

Hodgetts, R. M., Kuratko, D. F., & Hornsby, J. S. 1999. Quality implementation in small business: Perspectives from the Baldrige Award winners. *S.A.M. Advanced Management Journal*, 64 (1): 37–48.

Inc. 1999. The culture wars. May 18: 107.

Kanter, R. M. 1994. Collaborative advantage: The art of alliances. *Harvard Business Review*, 72 (4): 96–108.

Kanter, R. M. 1989. Becoming PALs: Pooling, allying, and linking across companies. *Academy of Management Executive*, 3 (3): 183–193.

Kaplan, R. S., & Norton, D. P. 1993. Putting the balanced scorecard to work. *Harvard Business Review*, 71 (5): 134–147.

Kaplan, R. S., & Norton, D. P. 1992. The balanced scorecard: Measures that drive performance. *Harvard Business Review*, 70 (1): 71–79.

Kerr, S. 1975. On the folly of rewarding A, while hoping for B. *Academy of Management Journal*, 18: 769–783.

Kilmann, R. H. 1985. Five steps for closing culture-gaps. In Kilmann, R. H., Saxton, M. J., Serpa, R., & Associates (Eds.), *Gaining control of the corporate culture*, 351–369. San Francisco: Jossey-Bass.

Klein, A. S., Masi, R. J., & Weidner, C. K., II 1995. Organization culture, distribution and amount of control, and perceptions of quality. *Group & Organization Management*, 20 (2): 122–148.

Kraut, A. I., Pedigo, P. R., McKenna, D. D., & Dunnette, M. D. 1989. The role of the manager: What's really important in different management jobs. *Academy of Management Executive*, 3 (4): 286–293.

Levering, R., & Moskowitz, M. 2000. The 100 best companies to work for. *Fortune*, January 10: 82–84, 88, 90, 92, 96, 98, 102, 104, 109–110.

Main, J. 1992. How to steal the best secrets around. *Fortune*, October 19: 102–106.

Mann, F. C., & Williams, L. K. 1960. Observations on the dynamics of a change to electronic data-processing equipment. *Administrative Science Quarterly*, 5 (3): 217–256.

Mereau, P., & Labbe, E. 1997. Practices and technology transfer in quality and information technology. *Human Systems Management*, 16 (3): 195–201.

Meyer, C. 1994. How the right measures help teams excel. *Harvard Business Review*, 72 (3): 95–103.

Meyer, J. P., Paunonen, S. V., Gellatly, I. R., Goffin, R. D., & Jackson, D. N. 1989. Organizational commitment and job performance: It's the nature of commitment that counts. *Journal of Applied Psychology*, 74 (1): 152–156.

Mintzberg, H. 1994. The fall and rise of strategic planning. *Harvard Business Review*, 72 (1): 107–114.

Morgan, S., & Dennehy, R. F. 1997. The power of organizational storytelling: A management development perspective. *Journal of Management Development*, 16 (7): 494–501.

Motiwalla, L., & Fairfield-Sonn, J. W. 1998. Measuring the impact of expert systems. *Journal of Business & Economic Studies*, 4 (2): 1–17.

Ogilvie, J. R. 1986. The role of human resource management practices in predicting organizational commitment. *Group & Organization Studies*, 11 (4): 335–359.

Pine, B. J. II, & Gilmore, J. H. 1998. Welcome to the experience economy. *Harvard Business Review*, 76 (4): 97–105.

Pine, B. J. II, Peppers, D., & Rogers, M. 1995. Do you want to keep your customers forever? *Harvard Business Review*, 73 (2): 36–47.

Porter, M. E. 1996. What is strategy? *Harvard Business Review*, 74 (6): 61–78.

Prahalad, C. K., & Hamel, G. 1990. The core competence of the corporation. *Harvard Business Review*, 68 (3): 79–91.

Prahalad, C. K., & Krishman, M. S. 1999. The new meaning of quality in the information age. *Harvard Business Review*, 77 (5): 109–118.

Procopio, A. J., & Fairfield-Sonn, J. W. 1996. Changing attitudes towards quality: An exploratory study. *Group & Organization Management*, 21 (2): 133–145.

Prokesch, S. E. 1997. Unleashing the power of learning: An interview with British Petroleum's John Browne. *Harvard Business Review*, 75 (5): 146–148, 150, 152–158, 160, 162, 164, 166, 168.

Pyzkek, T. 1999. The value of six sigma. *Quality Digest*, 19 (12): 20.

Pyzdek, T. 1999. Six sigma is primarily a management program. *Quality Digest*, 19 (6): 26.

Raspa, R. 1990. The CEO as corporate myth-maker: Negotiating the boundaries of work and play at Domino's Pizza. In Gagliardi, P. (Ed.), *Symbols and artifacts: Views of the corporate landscape.* 273–279. Berlin: de Gruyter.

Reichheld, F. F., & Sasser, W. E., Jr. 1990. Zero defections: Quality comes to services. *Harvard Business Review*, 68 (5): 105–111.

Rucci, A. J., Kirn, S. P., & Quinn, R. T. 1998. The employee-customer profit chain at Sears. *Harvard Business Review*, 76 (1): 82–97.

Rucker, R. 1999. Six sigma at Citibank. *Quality Digest*, 19 (12): 28–32.

Sethia, N. K., & Von Glinow, M. A. 1985. Arriving at four cultures by managing the reward systems. In Kilmann, R. H., Saxton, M. J., Serpa,

R., and Associates (Eds.), *Gaining control of the corporate culture*. 400–420. San Francisco: Jossey-Bass.

Slear, T. 1999. Changing jobs, facing choices. *Fidelity Focus*, Winter: 18–21.

Taguchi, G., & Clausing, D. 1990. Robust quality. *Harvard Business Review*, 68 (1): 65–75.

Tarpley, N. A. 2000. What really happened at Coke. *Fortune*, January 10: 114–116.

Tichy, N. 1989. GE's Crotonville: A staging ground for corporate revolution. *Academy of Management Executive*, 3 (2); 99–106.

Treacy, M., & Wiersema, F. 1993. Customer intimacy and other value disciplines. *Harvard Business Review*, 71 (1): 84–93.

Trice, H. M., & Beyer, J. M. 1985. Using six organizational rites to change culture. In Kilmann, R. H., Saxton, M. J., Serpa, R., and Associates (Eds.), *Gaining control of the corporate culture*. 370–399. San Francisco: Jossey-Bass.

Weber, Y. 1996. Corporate cultural fit and performance in mergers and acquisitions. *Human Relations*, 49 (9): 1181–1202.

Zack, M. H., & McKenney, J. L. 1996. Social context and interaction in ongoing computer-supported management groups. *Organization Science*, 6 (4): 394–422.

Zeithaml, V. 1988. Consumer perceptions of price, quality, and value: A means-end model and synthesis of evidence. *Journal of Marketing*, 52 (7): 2–22.

Index

About the Author

JAMES W. FAIRFIELD-SONN is Associate Professor of Management at the Barney School of Business, University of Hartford. Voted Outstanding Teacher of the Year in 1999, he teaches courses in process management and leadership.